Interventions is produced on the land of the Wurundjeri people of the Kulin Nation. We acknowledge the Traditional Owners of country throughout Australia and recognise their continuing connection to land, waters and culture. We pay our respects to their Elders past, present and emerging. Their land was stolen, never ceded.

It always was and always will be Aboriginal land.

INTERVENTIONS

The dirty life of mining in Australia

A TRAVELOGUE

Lindsay Fitzclarence

INTERVENTIONS

Acknowledgement

I completed this book with the assistance of many people. I express my gratitude to the people of Interventions, particularly Janey Stone and Alexis James, for their interest in publishing the book and for subsequent support. I acknowledge the patient and thorough editorial work provided by Lisa Milner, the copy-editing skills of Eris Harrison and the design and layout work of Viktoria Ivanova. I also express my gratitude to Angela Osborne for her meticulous editing and search skills and for her genuine interest in the book's focus, and Sally Thomas who provided some early editorial input. Deakin University's Faculty of Arts and Education funded Angela's work and I thank Deakin for this support. Jane Kenway provided 'ruthless interventionist editorial support' and advice which helped bring the book to its final publication stages.

More generally I acknowledge the assistance of those who provided information and insights about the different mining communities that are central to this study. Finally, I thank family and friends who have offered support, encouragement, and interest in this project. I dedicate this book to my grandchildren Harry, Ava, Claire, Maggie, and Frankie.

All images in this book are mine.

First published 2023 by Interventions Publishers

Interventions Inc is a not-for-profit, independent, radical book publisher. For further information:
www.interventions.org.au
info@interventions.org.au
PO Box 963
Coffs Harbour NSW 2450

Design and layout by Viktoria Ivanova.
Cover design from photograph by Lindsay Fitzclarence.

Author: Lindsay Fitzclarence

Title: The Dirty Life of Mining in Australia: A Travelogue
ISBN: 978-0-6452535-4-2: Paperback

A catalogue record for this work is available from the National Library of Australia

Content

Starting out

In 2014, the BBC aired a television program titled *Supersized Earth: The Story of our Manmade World*,[1] a three-episode documentary that provides an overview of humans' impact on the planet, giving on-the-ground descriptions of large-scale changes. The synopsis summarises the documentary:

> In the last generation, we have changed the face of the Earth on a scale unimaginable to our ancestors... *Supersized Earth* showcases the extraordinary engineering, construction and farming ingenuity that is transforming Earth, propelling us into a new era in this planet's – and our own – history... we have revolutionised how we harness our food, our energy and our water. As our population has grown so too has our ambition. We have entered an unprecedented age... transforming the earth as never before... we've become a force of nature. Harnessing energy...we have created incredible man-made landscapes. We have shrunk our planet by moving faster and further... That incredible pace of change across the globe has been driven by our ability to make giant leaps beyond what we thought was feasible... combination(s) of imagination, ambition, creativity, technology are drawing up the blueprints for the future.[2]

The series was an unabashed celebration of humans' capacity to transform social, manufactured and natural environments. This transformation is occurring on a massive scale and with increasing speed. Such a celebratory perspective reflects an enduring and evolving faith in the idea of human progress. Understood this way, mining is an important part of this storyline of progress – a storyline that must be challenged.

Mining, as a mode of practice and production, has a long history. It offers the resources needed to sustain human life and to provide greater human security. Extracted materials have been used as tools, weapons, currency, sources of fuel and energy and for building machines and transmitting communications. Over time, the processes of locating, extracting, processing and distributing earth's materials have changed with the development of more efficient tools and techniques of production. In relatively recent times – during just the past two centuries – remarkable developments in science and technology have greatly advanced mining practices.

Gambrenk Mining Engineering provides an excellent overview of changes within mining and the changes that mining facilitates:

> we are now in a society that depends on automobiles, trains, and airplanes for transportation; telephones, and computers for communications; fertilizers and heavy machinery for our agricultural output; industrial minerals for home building products; and coal-fired and nuclear plants for our electrical power.[3]

Overall, this book critically scrutinises mining as a production process. Mining involves a structured workforce and functions as an extended industrial assemblage that operates within dynamic global markets. This means that minerals extracted in one location can end up as processed material in a production chain that finishes far away. Such processes are the outcome of economic exchanges that unite capital, industrial knowhow, a physical plant, extensive transport networks and marketing processes. This book offers various examples, distilling perspectives from the work of many theorists, commentators and activists – often quoting at length, because their views are so revealing. Two authors, Naomi Klein and Tony Birch, stand out, and Chapter 4 elaborates on their work. Many of their perspectives inform the direction of the book.

The core themes derived from these writers are spliced together here to form a meta-narrative about mining as an industry that has certain flow on effects that include serious problems and contradictions. This meta-narrative involves critical scrutiny of mining's industrial and commercial processes and land use practices. Indeed, the use and misuse of land is a major theme. Further, there are certain land use practices in remote areas which, although not involving extraction, draw on the same mindset as mining. I identify some such practices and show how notions of *terra nullius* inform them.

The spark

The impetus for this book was the 2014 wildfire which entered the open-cut brown coal mine at Hazelwood power station near Morwell – a small mining community in the Latrobe Valley of Victoria. Its smoky fallout was disastrous for the town, as Chapters 1 and 2 explain. While there is no doubt that members of the local community have felt the effects most directly and dramatically, the forces driving these developments are manifestations of much longer and larger logics and dynamics.

Taking a long view: this relatively small and obscure location has been subject to forces of change that have unfolded over a long time and are now stretching outwards around the globe. One example of this is the fact that the mining operations in Morwell and nearby Yallourn attracted large numbers of immigrant workers, mostly from Europe, during the post WWII economic boom.[4] During that postwar period, Australia's dominant English/Irish colonial demographic changed significantly in a series of waves of migration that continue to this day. Alongside and around such changes, profound political and economic developments combined to more closely integrate Australia's economy into the expanding global marketplace. Thus, for example, the power station and mine complex at Morwell/Hazelwood, initially established by the state of Victoria, was privatised. A company based in Paris now owns and controls it.

Paul Carter vividly describes the implications of such trends in his account of settlers of the Mallee region of Victoria. The following excerpt dramatises the role the labouring classes played in large-scale projects of 'nation' building:

> They are in the national consciousness little more
> than ghosts, necessary hypotheses to explain these
> comprehensive transformations of geography, but they are
> not counted – their painful labour, their children dying from
> a representative variety of illnesses.[5]

Carter's description could well apply to Australia's mining workers. He correctly identifies class-based dynamics and contradictions as important, although underrepresented, elements within the wider forces of globally expanding capitalism. He asserts:

> The labour performed on a land whose extent has been
> quantified and parcelled out in uniform units is a double
> labour, for the labourer working in these conditions has
> constantly to measure his performance against the abstract
> tyranny of a target or return – and these calculations come
> from somewhere else, from some celestial calculator of
> profit and loss. [6]

Such larger dynamics of change are evident in various forms in mining locations. Ultimately, they are the result of the practices and values built into the fabric of high-tech capitalism. My interest is in identifying these larger dynamics while also exploring their fine grain – their grounded expressions in place and space.

The Morwell catastrophe provoked me to ask about the effects and dangers of mining extraction in other locations in Australia.

In turn, this led me to undertake an eight-year project which involved journeying and journalling in several other mining centres. This book draws from my travels. But it is also rooted in my biography.

I have historical connections to Morwell. These have led me to feel deeply, but ambiguously, connected to its triumphs and troubles. I was born in Morwell and spent 17 years there before leaving to study in Geelong and Melbourne. At the time, I was glad to escape. But I regularly visited the town, because my parents and siblings still lived there. In 2002, I returned to Morwell to work at Monash University's Churchill campus. As a result of these deep and ongoing connections to place and people, I had come to normalise mining and the burning of coal. I simply accepted that it was a vital part of the structure of modern industrial production. I also knew, from firsthand experience, how invested the local community felt in mining and power production.

However, during my various visits, I experienced considerable dissonance and was provoked to think critically about many matters. These included, firstly, the viability and security of generating power by extracting and burning coal, a volatile fossil fuel. My second concern was about the risks and challenges for owners and managers of open pit mining in extreme weather conditions. Thirdly, I was especially concerned about the problems and risks facing a community located close to the edge of an open pit coal mine.

The journey begins

Later, after a period of extended reading about the history of coal mining in the Latrobe Valley and other locations, I planned a long trip to a selection of mining locations in New South Wales (NSW), South Australia (SA) and Western Australia (WA). I chose not to focus on coal mining, because that was central to Morwell; so, I included locations that mined iron ore, lead, silver, uranium, diamonds and gold.

My aim was to 'scope' the effects of mining on local communities, focusing on the interactions of three key aspects of the mining process: the workers and their families; the owners of the mining sites (Australian and multinational); and the State itself. In defining the State, I include the legislative powers of state and federal governments and the constitutional authority of the federal government.

I use the term 'scoping' to indicate that my inquires did not involve extended immersion in each location. Rather, I tried to develop a solid sense of each place, through what I call investigative visiting. I gathered information about each place, inspected the mines, talked to a range of people, collected printed material about the town and the mine, walked around observing all I could and took many photographs. I also wrote extensive notes in my journal. As I journeyed through these locations, I came to realise that my investigation involved much more than visitation and observation of mine sites and their economic linkages. It required a deep sensitivity to the politics and culture of place, people and local narratives. It necessitated stopping and taking time to look carefully, to listen intently and to be open to moments that were different, confronting and uncomfortable. Edward Abbey, an American environmentalist and writer, has vividly expressed the value in activating such sensibilities:

> You can't see anything from a car; you've got to get out of the goddamn contraption and walk, better yet crawl, on hands and knees, over the sandstone and through the thornbush and cactus. When traces of blood begin to mark your trail, you'll see something, maybe. [7]

My trip through central and western parts of the country covered approximately 12,000 km and took just under two months. I visited mining communities in Broken Hill, Roxby Downs, the East Kimberley, Newman and Kalgoorlie. I discuss these in Part Three. I also visited various places in between each of my main locations; I discuss these in Part Four.

This project involved three major, intertwined research journeys – *material*, *ontological* and *educational*. I take the reader with me on these three journeys.

The *material journey* included the investigative visiting noted above and the time on the road between the five mining communities – important liminal spaces that shed additional light. Behind the wheel of my vehicle, I had plenty of time to think about the sites and the spaces between them. To deepen my insights, I later took some side trips in WA, Victoria and Tasmania. I revisited Kalgoorlie several times and took weekend study trips to the mining communities of Collie and Greenbushes, both located south of Perth. In Victoria, I returned to Morwell and also studied the closure of the brown coal mine at Anglesea, south of Geelong. In Tasmania, I went to Queenstown and the Mt Lyall mine. Except for Anglesea, I have not included discussions of these subsequent locations. Anglesea was particularly interesting because it was in the process of closure and rehabilitation.

The second major journey was *ontological*. The project changed me. When I drove away from the urban centres in the south-east of the continent, I travelled into highly politicised spaces. The further I travelled, the more complex and confronting this experience became. The longer I was away from the security and relative comforts of home, and the more time I had to reflect on my experiences, the more I had to put my own perceptions, assumptions and prejudices under pressure. I was constantly provoked to review and renew my sense of self, my sense of place and my sense of self in place.

The third journey was *educational*. I delved deeply into a vast amount of related literature, including government policies, company reports and assorted commentary about the political economy of mining. This helped me to learn more about the industrial and legal configurations of mine ownership, mine production methods and the politics of climate change, land ownership and land use.

Mining narratives

Large-scale mining has many links to the 'big end of town' in Australia. Fleming, Merrett and Ville[8] have charted the rise and rise of large corporations, including mining companies, in shaping and directing Australian economic life and politics. As a result, a cadre of corporation CEOs and a handful of mining advocacy groups have become the public narrators and spokes-people of the mining industry. For example, Michael Roche, in his role as Chief Executive of the Queensland Resources Council (2005–2016), was a very visible and active spokesper-son for mining as an industry and for its key institutions. He brought wide-ranging and high-level experience to that role – as Executive General Manager of the Australian Stock Exchange's markets and as Chief of Staff to the Queensland Treasurer and in Queensland's Cabinet Office.[9]

One of the authors of *The Big End of Town*, Simon Ville, fur-ther explored the prominence and power of peak body advo-cates in an Academy of Social Sciences presentation in 2014.[10] Early in the presentation, he asserted: 'Behind every policy strategy, of government or business, lies a narrative statement that contextualises and justifies a course of action'. He then posed a key question:

> Who develops these narratives and how well informed
> are they? We have many 'narrators' of the public
> discourse of economics, including the media, political
> parties, public sector bodies, business, and indeed
> universities – each with their own set of interests
> and values. Too often they develop narratives that
> are ahistorical or 'use' history to serve predetermined
> perspectives. Few would deny the media's power in
> influencing public opinion and policy makers…
> Australia has one of most concentrated business sectors
> in the developed world. The frequent public exhortations
> of captains of leading banking and mining firms are
> presented as though the apparent wisdom is held by only
> a few… Political parties and their backers have the power
> to implement policies but they still require a narrative
> to justify their actions. The narrative is shaped to
> reinforce their political philosophy and vested interests.
> Increasingly, the operations of the public service have
> also become politicised in pursuit of these narratives.

This comment about the evolution of narratives about mining offers a useful insight into the political power and influence of the Australian mining industry, as it becomes more deeply embedded in the practicalities of global capitalism – including the process of maintaining public legitimacy. Ville's commentary illuminates how its narratives can be mobilised and coordinated, how they spread, and how the mass media enables them to gain purchase with the public through the ongoing manipulation of myths, popular opinions and ignorance about the complex dynamics associated with Australia's mining industries. I draw on Ville's focus on narrative throughout, including his argument that changing the narrative is vital.

During the span of this study, the global climate crises were intensifying, as were the rebuttals by the climate change denialists.

The imperative of climate change

On 21 March 1994, the United Nations Framework Convention on Climate Change (UNFCCC) entered into force. The political and legislative element of the Framework is the Conference of Parties (COP), the primary decision-making body of the Convention.

In December 2015, 195 countries – including the USA – held the first meeting in Paris and adopted the Paris Agreement, aiming to prevent global temperatures from rising more than 1.5° C – 2° C above pre-industrial levels. This necessitated a reduction in the gases that enter the atmosphere, increase global warming and bring about climate change. Logically, power production plants involving the burning of fossil fuels, such as in the Latrobe Valley, were implicated in the short and long-term plans for change.

At the end of the COP 21 meeting in 2015, 185 countries signed up to a program limiting greenhouse emissions by 2025–2030. The USA's commitment involved a reduction in emissions of 26–28 percent by 2025. These outcomes were immediately reinforced when, on 1 January 2016, the United

Nations 2030 Agenda for Sustainable Development began. This was described as a 'road map' integrating three components in the process of monitoring and limiting emissions: economic, social and environmental. COP27, in Egypt, is underway as I write in 2022.

Behind the banner of this ongoing program is an assumption that rising global temperatures and increasing numbers of extreme weather events require urgent attention. At a more practical level, this is a warrant for greater use of renewable energy sources in moving towards a low-carbon future.

Within the realm of global climate crises, and the ever-growing sense of an escalating emergency, the signs are dire. The World Meteorological Organization produced the most recent report from the multi-sector coalition of climate scientists, *United in Science 2022*. Cryptically, this is a warning that the world is moving into 'uncharted territory of destruction'. The report highlights the signs that we have reached several tipping points. These occur once a critical global temperature is reached, and irreversible changes take hold. Key examples include the collapse of large regions of ice shelf, the warming of oceans and seas, marked anomalies in rainfall patterns over large areas of land and increasing numbers of periods of extreme heat in many locations. The alarming contradiction here is that, while the Australian Government willingly signs pro-environment treaties, it has a long and continuing history of supporting and underwriting mining throughout the nation. The constitutional ruling that gives authority to the states and territories to manage the developments and practices of the extended range of mining industries exacerbates the problem.

There is no room for complacency. Alternative narratives and practices are urgently necessary if we are to remedy the mistakes of the past. We must begin by acknowledging mining's ugly legacy. Clearly, the environmental damage mining causes must not be repeated. And colonisation via land acquisition and the extractive industries must end. Aboriginal and Torres Strait Islander people have experienced such colonisation for the past 234 years. They have had enough. Dominant understandings of appropriate land use must change and become more in tune with those of Indigenous people. Some costs, damage and destruction are documented in the following chapters. They demonstrate that the dirty life of mining cannot continue.

The Morwell mine pit during fire
of 2014, Victoria

PART ONE

Follow the Fire

'The world is undergoing multiple complex transitions: towards a lower-carbon future; towards technological change of unprecedented depth and speed; towards new global economic and geopolitical configurations. Managing these transitions and the deeply interconnected risks they entail will require long-term thinking, investment and international cooperation.'[1] As the world becomes more integrated and interconnected, who is responsible for managing such change – including those moments when there are major breakdowns? One major breakdown is fire.

1.
Choking on smoke: the Morwell mine fire

Land of the Kurnai language group

Jason Edwards is a natural history photographer. His work has taken him to all the continents, and his photographs have featured in media outlets in dozens of countries. In February 2014, while on his way to eastern Victoria, he found himself at the edge of a firestorm.[1] Forced to delay his trip, he began compiling a photographic record of the developing inferno. The fire, which had started between the towns of Moe and Morwell, had quickly raced through trees adjacent to a major freeway. Fanned by strong winds and moving east, it soon reached the edge of Morwell, threatening homes, infrastructure and industry on the perimeter of the town. Here, Edwards began photographing the drama, his images scoping the scale of the emergency. The portfolio of photos includes images of an emergency vehicle dwarfed by the flames; the main street of the town shrouded in billowing smoke; and firefighters battling to control the blaze many hours after it began.

For many people living elsewhere, far from this event, these photos and brief descriptions of the fire would have been a little update among many others that appear daily in the never-ending stream of mass media bulletins. In Morwell, however, and at the adjacent mine site and the Hazelwood power station, a different story was unfolding.

Efforts to stop the fire entering Morwell were largely

successful. After devouring a small number of houses and buildings, the fire was diverted from its easterly path along its northern perimeter. Unfortunately, this was not the case on the southern side, where the fire entered disused sections of the open-cut mine that fuelled the adjacent Hazelwood power station. Soon, the flames, sparks and embers spread throughout the massive coal field, creating an emergency that threatened the town, the power station and the associated power generation infrastructure, including coal-laden conveyor belts. Within a few hours, the fire had become a major threat to the energy supplies of the state of Victoria and – to a lesser extent – to the national electricity grid.

State Emergency Services were soon fully engaged in a major struggle with a firestorm that was beginning to rage unexpectedly. Intense heat from the burning coal caused the fires to roll and tumble – even to move upwards over steep slopes. This crisis on the mine's northern edge threatened the adjacent freeway, only a few metres away, as well as homes in the southern part of Morwell. In the strong updraft, carbon monoxide fumes streamed out of the mine and over the town. Meanwhile, on the opposite side of the mine, a different fire moved towards the massive power station.

For over a month, large numbers of fire crews and emergency management staff worked to contain, control and extinguish the fire. During that time, many residents were forced to leave their homes for other locations. Houses, shops and buildings were covered: invaded by ash and shrouded in polluted and toxic air. Helicopters carrying large water buckets dropped their loads on the hot spots, and fire-retarding foam covered burning coal seams. Firefighters, subject to these extreme conditions, were forced to endure health-threatening circumstances. Not until 25 March was the fire area declared 'safe'.

Meanwhile, as the firefighters fought to control the blaze, a virtual firestorm engulfed the region – created by competing political interests and fuelled by the mass media. A short piece distributed by Reuters in the first week of March 2014 provides a useful entrée into the narrative being constructed by the media.[2] Journalists Maggie Lu Yueyang and Stuart McDill reported on the fire emergency that had seen vulnerable citizens urged to leave and face masks issued. They noted that such a fire emergency would rarely continue for over three weeks in a 'developed' nation. Their punchline was that no such 'developments' had occurred in northern India, where some coal fires had burned for generations.

News articles in the USA (*Newsweek*) and UK (*Daily Mail*) placed the fire on a global platform. Media outlets across Australia also gave the fire situation considerable coverage. As a result, people local to the Morwell region suddenly found multiple outlets for their reactions of anxiety, frustration, anger and fear. This cocktail of perspectives also included the 'experts' recruited to provide commentary; politicians using parliaments as a platform to offer judgements; and environment groups weighing in with analyses and arguments about the problems and dangers of coal-fuelled power stations. Akin to a military campaign, the 'emergency' was occurring on many different fronts.

My visit to Morwell, the mine and Hazelwood power station

Aided by the extensive media coverage, I was able to follow the unfolding developments of the drama in Morwell. Phone calls to friends and acquaintances living in the region also provided telling insights about what was happening. One exchange remains vivid. A friend who worked at Hazelwood power station told me that, from his vantage point in the power station, he witnessed the fire entering the mine. He said that he had long feared such an event and believed that the company was under-resourced to cope with the critical emergency. He reported that the local grapevine suggested that an arsonist had started the fire.

On 9 March 2014, I drove from Melbourne to Morwell to witness the events firsthand. From a high vantage point above the Yallourn Power Station and open-cut mine, I looked across at Morwell, the Hazelwood power station and the mine. From there, I could observe smoke and ash drifting across the valley. Smog and smoke shrouded Morwell and the Hazelwood power station. Water-bombing helicopters were just visible, working along the edge of the smouldering coalface. Outside this epicen-tre of the emergency, burnt plantations acted as reminders of the pathway and intensity of the fires on the roads into Morwell.

Many years ago, Morwell and its power works were described to me as forming a 'reverse oasis'. The suggestive force of that label came back to mind as I looked down on the town and its power station. By my reasoning, a reverse oasis would be a harsh, unforgiving environment in the middle of a lush and fertile re-gion. This perverse label resonated with my enduring memories of the town, activating thoughts of grey, smog-filled skies and the constant deep throbbing of big turbines setting yet more machines in motion. However, beyond the town to the south lay the green, rolling hills of the Strzelecki Ranges; to the north, the blue, forest-covered peaks of the Great Dividing Range; and, to the east, the expansive wonderland of the Gippsland Lakes. From the lookout high on the ridge above the valley, this cocktail of thoughts, memories and feelings returned to me.

Entering the fire zone, I travelled to the Hazelwood power station and the management nerve centre for the firefighting teams. The carpark housed dozens of firefighting vehicles and equipment, waiting in readiness in case the heat and dry winds returned and spread the fire across the whole coalfield. Deep within the mine and on the northern perimeter opposite the power station, firefighters continued their work to control and contain the fire. Meanwhile, it was business as usual at the pow-er station: turbines rumbled, and smoke emerged from several of the chimneys. Watching the smoke billow up and into the atmosphere, I mused on Hazelwood's reputation as Australia's most polluting power station – that also generated 25 percent of the state's base electricity requirements. This tension led environment groups and their legions of activists to campaign for Hazelwood's closure and replacement by alternative clean energy production.

Another lookout at the extreme eastern edge of the coalfield provided a good view of activity within the huge 1,000-hectare basin. I observed large dredgers working deep in the pit, well away from the fire zone. Meanwhile, along one remote corner of the mine, the decommissioned area had clearly been closed off and left idle, its water-spraying system dismantled. Regarding the scene, I recalled being confused as a very young child by the sight of large areas of the open-cut mine being kept wet during summer. Over time, I came to understand the importance of this practice in safeguarding against fire.

The decision to dismantle the mine's watering system defied both logic and the lessons of the history of the region. The Latrobe Valley has a long legacy of rapidly moving wildfire. Since European colonial settlement in the mid-19th century, runaway fires have destroyed lives and property on several occasions. In 1944, a fire raced across the floor of the valley and then over the Strzelecki Ranges to the south. Twelve people died, hundreds of properties were destroyed, and the Yallourn minefield was threatened. In the street where I lived during my school years, several houses had been burned in the 1944 fire. Most recently, in February 2009, a fire not far from Hazelwood's mine killed 11 people, destroyed 145 houses and burned 25,000 hectares of land.

From the mine lookout, I drove into Morwell. The town has traditionally serviced the local power industries: the Hazelwood power station, the former Morwell power station, the Energy Brix power station and the Lurgi Gasification plant. After a period of growth and relative community prosperity, the privatisation of energy production had taken a toll on the region. The signs of economic downturn and struggle were visible in the condition of many houses and the number of 'For Sale' signs.

From a vantage point on the town's main shopping strip, I could look directly across the mine and onto the imposing structure of the Hazelwood power station. Although the smoke from the fire partly obscured my view, I remembered just how close the power station and the mine are to the southern part of the town. From this position, I also observed that the streets and the central shopping centre were almost free of vehicles, pedestrians and normal activity. The town was in lockdown.

The Rose Garden is one of Morwell's few aesthetic landmarks, highlighted as a showcase for visitors in profiles of the town. For many years, residents, including my mother, worked to establish and maintain the beautiful garden. During my visit, I returned to the Rose Garden for a ritual walk, only to find the glorious flowers covered in grit and grime left by the smoke and ash.

Driving to the Morwell football oval, I knew that I was close to where Jason Edwards had taken his photographs of the fire at the edge of the town. The oval is only a short distance from the northern edge of the mine, as the crow flies. Despite the smoke still pluming up out of the coalfield, I had a close-up view of the helicopters dropping bucketloads of water on the fire. I also met and talked with the groundsman. Ironically, he was in good spirits and happy to stop work and share his thoughts about the events of the previous month. He told me that he had been working at the oval when the fire started. He described his observations and feelings as the fire came to within several hundred metres of where he was working. He expressed gratitude for the efforts of the firefighters who struggled to stop the inferno entering the town – sentiments no doubt shared by many others – and voiced his relief at being able to resume his normal work because the fire was close to being controlled. I thanked him for his story and drove on, feeling relieved that I had encountered one person whose sense of normality was beginning to return.

On 11 March, two days after my visit, authorities declared the fire 'under control'. Subsequently, on 25 March, the state's Fire Commissioner, Craig Lapsley, announced that the fire had been 'one of the largest, longest running and most complex fires in the State's history'.[3]

2.
Shifting blame: struggles over responsibility

When disasters occur, it is now standard procedure to conduct an inquiry. The many reasons for this include satisfying a need for public accountability and shaping and controlling the political agenda. A comprehensive examination facilitates a narrative about what happened before and during an event, then helps to set an agenda for future changes and policy development. The Morwell fire inquiry maintained this trend. On 21 March 2014, four days before the fire had been officially declared under control, the state's Governor in Council announced an inquiry.

Over the next five months, a three-person panel conducted hearings, gathered information and assembled a report. The investigation focused on questions about the origin and circumstances of the event; the management and effectiveness of GDF Suez's response; related matters of compliance to regulations and laws; and the adequacy and effectiveness of emergency services and government agencies in addressing the health and wellbeing needs of local residents.

The report was conducted and presented within an abbreviated time frame. A state election was due by the end of the year. This meant that the inquiry occurred in the shadow of many competing political interests and influences operating at local, regional and state levels. The commissioners' task was undoubtedly more complex because of the pressure and the large number of elements to be identified, investigated and integrated into a coherent set of conclusions and recommendations. Under such circumstances, it seems inevitable that the inquiry would produce controversial findings, unsatisfactory conclusions and inadequate recommendations.

The Victorian Governor received the final document, 430 pages in length, on 29 August 2014. After its publication, concerns and criticisms about the content were immediate. In the first week of September 2014, *The Weekly Times* published details of negative reactions by a local action group, Voices of the Valley, representing people from the region. Concerns included: that the report was 'weak' in addressing the health situation of many residents; that it failed to provide recommendations about their health problems; and that it lacked detail about necessary follow-up procedures for those affected by the fire. A related concern involved its 'superficial' acknowledgement of many pre-existing health problems within the community. The body of the report did provide detailed consideration of health issues, but this did not follow through into the recommendations, fuelling many of these negative responses. Significantly, the Australian Labor Party (ALP), then in Opposition, quickly supported the claims of Voices of the Valley and gave an undertaking to address the matter if the ALP won office at the upcoming state election. The ongoing management of the mine fire was suddenly propelled into the realpolitik of the time.

On 29 November 2014, Victorian voters elected a new state government. In a two-party preferred result, the ALP unseated the Liberal–National Coalition to take office. In the seat of Morwell District, the Nationals candidate, Russell Northe, retained his seat after experiencing a swing against him of 11.5 percent. An independent candidate, Tracie Lund, polled 10.91 percent of the votes, receiving strong support from the voting locations most directly affected by the smoke and pollution of the fire. Antony Green, political analyst and media commentator, surmised that the poll reflected concerns about:

the mishandling of the fire in the Morwell open-cut early in 2014, and the town of Morwell being shrouded in acrid smoke for several weeks.[1]

The commissioners had confronted myriad challenges, stretching across many layers of concerns, influences and vested interests. Along with the pressure to investigate and publish within a short time frame was the problem of reaching conclusions about an important service industry. At the time, with Hazelwood power station providing 25 percent of the state's energy supply, the fire placed at risk the consistent supply of power essential for the state's economy.

A disaster of this kind threatens the stability of many facets of everyday life, well beyond its immediate location. It disrupted a mix of domestic, industrial and administrative processes. For this reason, analysis of the political flow on effects needs to be expansive and to incorporate local, regional and statewide considerations.

Five months after taking office, in May 2015, the new Labor government announced that they would reopen the Hazelwood Mine Fire Inquiry.[2] Influenced by pressure groups such as Voices of the Valley, the new inquiry committed to investigate:

> concerns of a spike in deaths following the fire, as well as the option of mine rehabilitation at all three coal mines in the Latrobe Valley – Hazelwood, Yallourn and Loy Yang.[3]

In this political arm wrestle, the next move came from utility owners GDF Suez. In early July 2015, a spokesperson announced that the company was not prepared to pay an account of $18 million for recovery costs, presented earlier in the year by the Country Fire Authority (CFA). This politics of resistance was justified on the grounds that the company made contributions to a fire services levy that:

> is in effect an insurance policy...designed specifically to cover fire suppression activities, whether they be large or small... We therefore don't believe it is fair, reasonable or

The last puffs of smoke from Hazelwood Power Station, on the day of its closure.

within the scope of applicable regulations for the CFA to seek further payment from [GDF Suez].[4]

A Supreme Court ruling in May 2020 resolved the matter of payment for the costs of managing the fire. Several utilities, working on behalf of the company, were charged a total of almost $2 million. The fine was a recovery for health and safety breaches and for the effects of pollution created by the fire. Environment groups were quick to point out the glaring discrepancy between the relatively small fine and the costs of fighting the fire and cleaning up after it. Other members of local advocacy groups also noted the inadequacy of the fine, given the ongoing health problems generated by the fire and the associated airborne pollution.

There is an important backstory to this announcement. In late April 2015, Gerard Mestrallet, Chair and CEO of GDF Suez, announced that the company was changing its brand name to ENGIE. Mestrallet explained:

> the world of energy is undergoing profound change… characterized by decarbonisation and the development of renewable energy sources… ENGIE. It is an easy name and one that is powerful, a name that evokes energy for everyone and in all cultures, a name embodying our values and activities. We thus confirm our new ambition and the dynamics of change that drive our Group… ENGIE upholds that energy is everyone's business: employees, shareholders, partners and customers, because collectively we are energy's architects. We are called upon to act together, to be optimistic, and seek solutions that will change the daily lives of everyone and bring the benefit of greater energy efficiency.[5]

There are many ways to interpret this statement. Firstly, it is a global and universal pitch, embracing an optimistic vision of a cleaner, healthier environment for everyone. It speaks on behalf of current generations and those yet to come. Secondly, it is an argument for a movement away from older, less efficient and more expensive modes of power production. This can be read as an address to company stakeholders and a demographic of 'alternatives' investors. Thirdly, these words seem designed to project an air of optimism about the future at a time when so many negative messages are circulating about the politics of power production.

Mestrallet's rhetorical flourishes did not bode well for the future of Hazelwood power station and its associated industries and employees. For over a decade before his announcement, Hazelwood had been labelled a polluting pariah. Images of its large, austere structure with its eight chimneys had become symbols of the generation of dirt, damage and atmospheric destruction. This negative branding of Hazelwood in the national and international politics of climate change created problems for a company involved in remaking its image within the global marketplace of power production. In March 2016, Isabelle Kocher, who was about to replace Gerard Mestrallet as Chair and CEO of ENGIE, began the public process of tolling the bell for Hazelwood when she forecast the company's switch to renewables and indicated that there would be no further developments in new coal projects. Seven months later, in November 2016, ENGIE announced Hazelwood's shutdown by the end of March 2017.

The fire burned for 45 days and had a significant impact on the lives of many residents – power production workers and emergency management personnel, including firefighters and health care workers. Two formal inquiries highlighted several issues, including:

- long-term health and safety issues for residents of Morwell and other Latrobe Valley communities who were located close to open pit coal mines
- the inadequacy of existing fire prevention measures adopted by the mine's owner
- the extent to which the follow up to these issues has had any tangible effect on mine management practices in the Latrobe Valley or elsewhere in the state and nation
- the lack of clarity about the primary responsibility for monitoring the mine owner's compliance through

regulations designed to prevent pit fires; to fight and control fires; and to preserve the safety and wellbeing of the local community, especially those most at risk, including the elderly, infirm and school children

- the adequacy of the advice provided by authorities to the residents of the communities most affected by the fire.

Considering the subsequent closure of Hazelwood power station and the associated loss of work for many employees, it is very difficult to quantify the complex amalgam of costs associated with this episode.

Much is not in plain sight in Morwell. This was the case when ownership of the mining processes passed from the State into the vagaries of the global marketplace, eventually leading to ownership by a French mega corporation. Certainly, the latent contradictions and dangers associated with management at a distance by bureaucrats based in Paris are not immediately evident. The myriad transactions involved in extracting profit often occur out of sight – with local people out of mind.

How are we to comprehend the multiple, but often impenetrable, dynamics at work here? How are they best named? I have coined the term 'configurations of extraction' to help address these questions.

These have the following core components: mines and markets, workers and owners/controllers, technologies and ideologies and governments. Each part changes over time, and so do the interactions between them. The parts, and the whole, are thus regularly reconfigured. Configurations of extraction have many components: some territorial and some de-territorialised, some embodied and others disembodied, some highly visible, others much less visible. Further, their various components operate on different scales – they are multiscalar. Many contemporary configurations of extraction can be considered global because some of their parts operate on that scale – particularly their owner/controllers, their markets and their technologies.

Mining in Morwell can certainly be understood in this way, as can mining in the locations discussed in the following chapters.

PART TWO

Thinking Mining, Mining Thinking

3.
Australian mining: dominant and subordinate narratives

Dominant narratives and narrators

In March 2019, *Mine Australia Magazine* featured an article by J. P. Casey, 'Super mines: Australia's biggest mining projects'. It profiled the piece:

> From a mine built atop the world's largest uranium deposit to a project producing close to a million ounces of gold per year, Australia is home to some of the world's largest and most ambitious mining projects.[1]

Casey writes:

> Australia boasts some of the world's largest mineral deposits, including 21.9 billion tonnes of iron ore and 3,550 tonnes of gold, stretched over one of the largest and most sparsely populated islands in the world. With just 3.1 people per square kilometre, Australia has the seventh-lowest population density of any country on Earth, and there is considerable space for large-scale mining.

> With surface operations at Fimiston covering more than five
> square kilometres, and expansion work at the Boddington
> operation involving three times as much steel as was used
> to build the Eiffel Tower, these giant projects have been
> the cornerstone of the Australian mining sector, which
> contributed over $35bn to the country's GDP in 2018.[2]

The Fimiston pit mine in Kalgoorlie (WA), also known as the
Super Pit, is 3.5 km long, 1.5 km wide and almost 600 metres
deep. Until recently, it was Australia's largest open pit gold mine.
That title has now passed to a tri-corporation project involving
a copper and gold mine located near Bannister, approximately
100 km south-east of Perth WA. These two mining operations
are useful signifiers of the economic size and wealth generation
of mining, as an industry, in Australia.

In Casey's brief quote, we have a condensed version of the
mining industry's dominant narrative: Australia has vast deposits of minerals within a large, sparsely populated land mass.
Through a combined process of discovery, extraction, processing and exporting, mining makes a major contribution to the
nation's collective wealth generation.

This view of Australia – as a vast land-space containing
large amounts of minerals for the taking and unlimited scope
for myriad land use activities – has deep ideological roots.
At the most basic level, the paired activities of agriculture
and mining provide the foundations of Western civilisation.
However, also embedded in Casey's overview is the more insid-
ious belief system of the Doctrine of Discovery, a multifaceted
justification for claiming and colonising territory deemed to
be uninhabited.

The doctrine emerged in 1493 from a Catholic Church
edict and became enshrined within European political practice, with its penchant for colonising territory deemed to
be *terra nullius*. The Doctrine of Discovery underpins many
aspects of Australia's history as a British colony. From it
evolved many ideas, beliefs, practices, legalised precedents
and myths about Australia and Australians. The mass media
have perpetuated these.

Stereotypes, constantly repackaged over time, have helped to establish and maintain myths about the typical Australian male character, with behaviour showcased in war, sporting contests, outdoor exploits and achievements and – in current times – entrepreneurial successes. I am in contrast making a case for a critical examination of social and economic practices that are designed to glamourise and gloss over the harsh realities of the myth of *terra nullius* and the beliefs and practices of the Doctrine of Discovery.

In September 2015, the Australian Mining Industry held its inaugural Annual Lecture in Melbourne. It attracted a full house of around 300 participants. Historian Professor Geoffrey Blainey delivered the keynote address.

The Introduction involved two separate statements. Firstly, the CEO of the Minerals Council of Australia (MCA), Brendan Pearson, offered a general welcome. Pearson stressed the importance in public policy of a relevant and accurate account of 'context and historical perspective'. His rationale for this focus was the need to hold to account the mining industry's narrow-minded enemies and their short memories.

MCA Chairman Andrew Michelmore, introducing Professor Blainey, talked about Australia's mining industries as a tribe of members connected through 'affinity and empathy with mining and the role it has played in national life'. He asserted that tribes are defined, shaped and nourished by their storytelling; to that end, the mining industry and those present, were fortunate to have with them 'our most distinguished mining historian, a man who stands alone in the pantheon of scholars, the "Bradman" of our historians'.[3] Sir Donald Bradman is considered the greatest batsman to have played cricket at the highest level with his batting average far above any of his closest rivals, and comparison to him is the highest praise.

The significance of these introductions is that they clearly position Blainey as an insider to the extended mining community and highlight the importance of skilled orators in promoting industries and their peak bodies – in this case, the MCA.

Blainey – a mining industry insider

Blainey's talk, *Mining and the Australian people – the long view*, highlighted five major themes: Australians' widespread ignorance about mining; the historical contribution of mining; growing political hostility, evidenced by the proposed mining super-tax; the contribution of great mining companies to Australia's wealth and status; and the bravery of miners themselves.

Blainey reinforced Pearson's pitch about Australians' widespread ignorance about the mining industry and the work of the MCA. Eighty percent of Australia's population lives on the 'boomerang coast' – the eastern and southern coasts – removing most Australians from the realities of mining. Blainey fleshed out this observation by asserting that the realities of changes in mining had not filtered through to 90 percent of the population: most people do not understand that Australia now produces three times more gold annually than it did during the best years of the fabled gold rush period of the 1850s and 1860s.

Blainey stressed the importance of mining to the overall development of the different colonies during the second half of the 19th century. In an extended narrative, which also showcased his prodigious historical knowledge, he provided examples of the impact of the discovery of mineral deposits in the development of mining communities in far-flung regions of the continent. This geographic account then highlighted how, in post-federation times, successive prime ministers had direct links and affinities with mining. In a remarkable display of an encyclopaedic command of detail, he accounted for one prime minister after another, up to and including Robert Menzies's second time in office, which ended in 1966.

At this point in his historical sweep, Blainey sharpened his focus He noted a break in the knowledge and sympathies of contemporary politicians. His evidence of this development was the debates and legislation associated with the attempt to introduce a mining super-tax. Blainey asserted that none of those former prime ministers, with their intimate knowledge about coalfields and goldfields, would have drafted such legislation. Within the overall arc of the evening's presentation, this statement linked closely with Pearson's comment about mining's narrow-minded enemies with short memories.

According to Blainey, the discoverers of major coal and goldfields in Australia were heroes. He named three prime candidates: Charles Rasp at Broken Hill, Paddy Hannan in Kalgoorlie and Campbell Miles in Mount Isa. They were industrious pioneers attuned to their surroundings, risk takers with foresight about economic possibilities and industrial strategies. The story of Broken Hill, which evolved to become Broken Hill Proprietary Ltd (BHP), stands out as a flag bearer in Blainey's narrative. The fabulously rich deposits of silver and lead, discovered by Rasp and leased by company stockmen, represent 'one of the great stories in Australian history, not only in mining and business history but in the general history of Australia'.[4] Blainey summarised the evolution of BHP from its humble beginnings, under the control of stockmen from the Riverina, into the powerhouse global corporation that it is today.

He concluded with a tribute to the bravery of miners, who have worked in dangerous conditions. Many have paid the ultimate price in fires, explosions and floods. Fortunately, the work is now much safer than in the past. A legacy, however, can be read in Australians' bravery in wartime. During the two World Wars, Australian soldiers in locations around the world, including Gallipoli, showcased behaviour and attitudes developed in their civilian life through their work – specifically, in mining. Blainey always appealed to the national spirit.

Naomi Klein has described Francis Bacon as a patron saint of the extractive economy.[5] She awarded him this status because his writing and talks were designed to shift public positions towards humans as earth's masters. In contemporary and local terms, Geoffrey Blainey qualifies as an antipodean patron saint of the extractive economy.

For over 60 years, Blainey has been writing, celebrating, advocating and working for Australia's mining industries. For most of this time, he has enjoyed a virtual monopoly on the shaping of the history of mining in this country. His books, *The*

Peaks of Lyell[6] and *The Rush That Never Ended*,[7] have both been republished multiple times.

Writer Malcolm Knox is best known for his volumes on sport. It was, therefore, something of a curiosity that he would publish in 2013 an account of changes in mining in Australia. Knox describes his book, *Boom*, as:

> an attempt to put up and test the hypothesis that mining is…integral to Australians' perception of themselves; that mining is, in a metaphorical sense, woven into the national DNA.[8]

Knox's use of a molecular substance, DNA, as a metaphor to describe trans-social and cultural features of human existence provides an alternative to Blainey's more general and surface level story of mining.

DNA is a chemical substance associated with genetic inheritance, discovered in 1869. It took a further 74 years for the role of DNA in determining the form and function of the basic building blocks of life to be understood. Knox implies that the history of DNA is like that of mining in that it has taken a long time to be properly understood. He thus extends and deepens the existing storyline. If Knox is correct about the deeply entrenched and common mindset, the subsequent questions are: 'why is this so?' and: 'how do social, cultural and political processes combine to facilitate the process?' Take some everyday examples.

Australia's current national anthem offers a storyline highlighting several dominant themes. The line, 'We've golden soil and wealth for toil' foregrounds the importance of 'the land', including what exists within it. The line, 'Our land abounds in nature's gifts of beauty rich and rare' gestures towards the value that exists within the land. These themes are reinforced in a government statement explaining the reasons for selecting green and gold as the nation's choice of sporting colours. Governor-General the Honourable Sir Ninian Stephen formally recognised green and gold as the national colours – with widespread community support – on 19 April 1984.[9] The Department of Prime Minister and Cabinet noted that the national colours have strong environmental connections. Gold conjures images of Australia's beaches, mineral wealth, grain harvests and the fleece of Australian wool. Green evokes the forests, eucalyptus trees and pastures of the Australian landscape.

Dominant narratives can be distilled into catchwords or phrases that contain a host of assumptions. Take, for example, the more recent notion that Australia is the 'lucky country'. Originally, it was used by the writer Donald Horne to send up a cohort of politicians he considered second rate. However, the phrase has subsequently been used to describe Australia's good fortune in being distant from many of the world's political hot spots and arenas of conflict; having abundant natural resources; and enjoying a climate that is generally relatively mild – until recently – and free from the extremes of many other locations.

The dominant narrative's origins

Common narratives of the importance of mid-19th century gold rushes exemplify such themes. This storyline includes and unites information about population growth, social and political modernisation, expansion of the economic base and the movement towards national independence. All these themes are identifiable within an overview of gold mining in Victoria during the second half of the 19th century.

In 1850, gold was discovered near Clunes in the Central Highlands of Victoria. Prospectors seeking their fortunes arrived in large numbers. During this initial stage, the basic items of equipment were a cradle and metal pan. Shortly after the initial discovery, miners, speculators and investors began to form companies as more sophisticated mining techniques were developed. An example of this subsequent stage was the process of 'puddling' conducted on large leases of land: horse-driven equipment stripped, raked and washed the surface earth. One consequence of this technique was the pollution of local waterways by the 'overburden' – the waste.

Greater understanding about the geology of regions inspired more complicated and extensive methods of extraction. In the

Bendigo area, miners excavated quarries as a first step in exposing quartz reefs. They then sank shafts and opened tunnels to keep track of the deeper reefs. New machinery broke and sifted the excavated soil. In the Ballarat region, where gold-bearing seams were further underground, miners designed and employed deep shafts, using practices and techniques that had been developed in Wales, Cornwall and Scotland.

A range of techniques designed to store and move water throughout the diggings ran in tandem with these developments. A prime example of this work occurred with the construction of approximately 400 km of water races and one large storage pond in the area around Talbot, north of Ballarat. Other technologies soon followed. The development of machinery such as the rock drill enabled miners to dig more deeply and to install more intricate shafts while following gold-bearing seams through different rock strata.

After the initial flurry of activity created by the discovery of gold in Victoria's Central Highlands, gold mining began to morph into the shape and function of industries in the mainstream of the colonial economy. Financiers established companies that assembled experts, such as chemists and engineers, to sustain and advance processes of extraction. The Port Phillip Company, based in Clunes between Ballarat and Bendigo, is an excellent example. The initial finance for this company came from London. Over a 40-year period, the company extracted gold worth over £400,000.

During the 1850s, Victoria's population increased almost eightfold. This growth became a catalyst for multiple forms of change; the regions were transformed from small pastoral settlements into large and expanding regional cities. This growth pattern was amplified in the major gold mining regions, such as Ballarat, where the population increased from an estimated 1,000 in 1850 to approximately 50,000 by the late 1860s. With these changes came many commercial, administrative and legal developments. Road and rail networks were built, and municipal infrastructure was established and maintained. According to details from Australia's most recent census in 2021, the population of the Greater Bendigo region is 167,764; Ballarat's population is 173,937.

On a related but different level, the gold rushes of the mid-19th century became a springboard for several important political and workforce developments and reforms. One notable example was a process named 'tributing', which involved groups of miners working together in one part of a mine on the basis that they paid the owners a certain proportion of the gold that they extracted. A more specific example of worker solidarity and activism occurred in December 1854, when miners in Ballarat fought with local police and British troops in a protest against the imposition and collection of a 30 shillings per month miners' fee. On 3 December 1854, the civil unrest and resistance among the miners led to a confrontation between them and a relatively large and well-armed contingent of troops and police. In the conflict, 27 people died. This event, now known as the Eureka Stockade, generated a great deal of public support for the miners and resulted in changes to licensing practices; it also risked increased public support for greater political independence from British governance and for colonial home rule. In this sense, the unrest and dissatisfactions that culminated in the confrontation at the Eureka site helped to set the stage for the federation of colonies on 1 January 1901.

Mining emerged in tandem with the development of Australia as a modern, sovereign nation. And mining has become enmeshed with significant national songs, symbols and events.

Subordinate narratives

The dominant narrative about the significance of the gold rush era has glossed over, ignored or misrepresented many issues. Some of the themes linked to the subordinate narratives continue to resonate.

Industrial relations

The extreme excitement of individuals rushing to get to, and begin work on, the goldfields of Victoria's Central Highlands quickly evolved into forms of industry that were more in keeping with the factory systems of major cities. Companies arose backed by external funding, sometimes from overseas. Company based hierarchies of financiers, managers, workplace coordinators and labourers followed. Such divisions of labour produced many workplace struggles and abuses. At the same time, they set in motion dynamics that kickstarted the union movement in Australia.

Environmental damage

Environmental damage to land and waterways became a legacy of mining in the Central Highlands. This region, like other major mining locations, has many abandoned mine shafts and associated tunnels. The environmental changes caused by alluvial and deep lead mining were profound.

Gold mining was the second wave of catastrophic environmental degradation to impact on Victoria since European colonisation. The first phase was the pastoral period, effectively beginning in 1835. The landscapes that miners viewed were not, therefore, pristine – though they were often portrayed this way in writings and artwork. Miners seldom acknowledged that they were, in fact, part of the second wave of environmental devastation, let alone the dispossession of Indigenous people.[10]

Health and safety issues for workers

Mining was always, and continues to be, dangerous work. An examination of the extended region that has been the focus of this chapter highlights this issue. In December 1882, one of Australia's worst ever mine disasters occurred at the New Australasian No. 2 Deep Lead Gold Mine near Creswick.

On 11 December 1882, 41 men entered the New Australasian No. 2 mine to work a seemingly ordinary Monday night shift. In the early hours of Tuesday morning, 12 December 1882, water flooded the mine from the old workings of Australasian No. 1 mine, trapping 27 men underground. Rescue efforts commenced immediately; but, by the time rescuers reached the miners three days later, only five had survived.[11]

Since the time of this tragedy, hundreds of miners in many locations have perished while doing their work or because of injury or illness sustained while mining. Many mining locations have constructed honour boards – for example, the Miners' Memorial at Kalgoorlie, officially opened in 2014. It is a memorial wall inscribed with the names of over 1,400 miners who died in mining accidents or because of mine work in the Eastern Goldfields of WA.

Land rights issues

It is important for this composite story to include the role and experiences of Indigenous people, so often glossed over in existing stories about countless mining locations throughout the nation. The myth of Australia as the *terra nullius* continent has helped to gloss over, ignore, subvert and hide the hard facts of frontier conflicts and massacres. From the colonisers' perspective, these events were designed to establish absolute sovereignty over territory.

In 1984, Charles Perkins, then Chairman of the Aboriginal Development Commission, referred to the tensions between mining interests and Aboriginal rights. These tensions, Perkins is quoted as saying:

> date back to those times of notoriety, not so long ago, when
> certain Aboriginal groups resisting European pressures on
> their land were simply swept aside... The deep and degrading
> cultural disruption, the assault of noise, dust and lost
> privacy, the loss of social integrity of Aboriginal groups,
> and the outrageously low return in the way of royalties,
> employment, and other benefits, have all formed part of the
> picture of the Australian development 'frontier'.[12]

4.
Critical considerations

My educational journey included exploring many thinkers across diverse fields of knowledge and activist practice. Two people stand out – Naomi Klein and Tony Birch. Both scrutinise mining practices through anti-capitalist and anti-colonial lenses. Klein takes a global perspective, and Birch focuses largely on Australia.

Naomi Klein is a Canadian journalist, columnist and author. Her many widely read publications include critiques of contemporary cultural change and sociopolitical practices. Released in 2014, *This Changes Everything: Capitalism vs the Climate* remains highly relevant to current debates about climate change. This book is a tour de force, ranging across many issues.[1]

Overall, Klein argues that the harsh realities and future perils of the changing climate require us to question the most fundamental assumptions and values of our contemporary economy and society. In a nutshell, she questions the viability of the entire capitalist system.

Klein's argument is built around several themes. Firstly, contemporary capitalism wages war on the planet's life forms, environments and ecosystems. Secondly, 'due to the corporate state power nexus',[2] the State is so tightly entangled with capitalism that it is fundamentally compromised. Thirdly, capitalism has developed and fuelled the beliefs and practices whereby human society tames, dominates and, ultimately, destroys nature. Given the current state of the climate and the planet, Klein argues that this economic model is no longer viable. She identifies the key features of contemporary capitalism that have led directly to the crisis of climate change.

Extractivism is one such feature. She is not talking about extraction, understood simply as the process of extracting natural resources from the earth and ocean to profit from them. She is drawing on the broad and critical notion of extractivism, which links the biophysical with the social and the depletion of nature with capital accumulation. Such depletion involves the draining of natural resources, the degradation of land and soil, the extinction of whole species, the loss of biodiversity and irreversible climate change. The capital accumulation involved is driven by notions of infinite exploitability and growth in multiple locations and on multiple scales.

Klein's use of the term extractivism contains several levels of meaning. The most literal and traditional is a reference to the process of locating and removing natural 'resources', such as minerals or gas, which are then used for domestic and commercial ends. The second level of meaning invokes a more obscure and less direct process, whereby transactions and exchanges occur in a process designed to extract value and profit. Theoretically, this leads back to Marx's distinction between 'use' and 'exchange' value. The mysterious element of the exchange process is created by its lack of direct visibility. Once a raw material is extracted from nature, processed and turned into a commodity, it enters a borderless network of linkages and relationships.

Klein identifies the key features of extractivism:

> Extractivism is a nonreciprocal, dominance-based relationship with the earth, one purely of *taking*.
>
> It is the opposite of stewardship which involves taking but *also taking care that regeneration and future life continue*.
>
> It involves the *reduction of life into objects* for the use of others giving them no integrity or value of their own – turning living complex ecosystems into 'natural resources'.

It also involves the *reduction of human beings* either into *labour* to be brutally extracted, pushed beyond limits, or, alternatively, into *social burden* problems to be locked out at borders and locked away in prisons or reservations. (My emphases).[3]

This is one way of describing a capitalist system that knows no bounds and that is driven by a frenetic and competitive drive for profit and corporate advantage, leading to ceaseless plundering of resources. This has history.

Extractivism has strong links to colonialism and civilisationism. Centres of empire saw the colonies as sources of supply. Their natural endowments were extracted to feed industrial development at the centre. Colonised peoples were seen as less than human – uncivilised. They mattered so little that they were denied their humanity, economies, cultures and land. Such mindsets are echoed in the contemporary imperialism of 'development'. Klein argues:

This toxic idea has always been intimately tied to imperialism, with disposable peripheries being harnessed to feed a glittering centre and is bound up with notions of racial superiority... The colonial mind nurtures the belief that there is always somewhere else to go to and exploit once the current site of extraction has been exhausted.

These logics link directly to Klein's notion of sacrifice zones. Here, she refers to the places and people that are readily sacrificed to satisfy the demands of 'the economy'. Sacrifice zones have certain features in common. They are 'poor places. Out-of-the-way places. Places where residents lack political power usually having to do with some combination of race language and class'.[4] These 'unlucky places...hinterlands wastelands, nowheres' are 'kept safely out of view' from those who reap the most benefits from extractavism.[5] They are invariably out of sight and out of mind for the beneficiaries. Extractivism is inextricably linked to social and geographical inequality.

For Klein, we must replace extractivism with 'stewardship'.

This involves reciprocity, regeneration and ensuring that the planet lives on for future generations. She highlights the endeavours of various anti-extractivist activists, including fossil fuel divestment (and reinvestment) movements and those involved in what she calls 'Blockadia'.[6] Blockadia describes local people taking action in many places where extractivist projects are underway. It is grassroots and increasingly broad based and interconnected globally. Hence, Klein says, it 'is not a specific location on a map but rather a roving transnational conflict zone'.[7]

Klein argues that those activating Indigenous land and treaty rights are an important part of the resistance to extractivism. She identifies many such successful struggles around the world. She further observes that many non-Indigenous people are starting to acknowledge two important matters: firstly, that 'these rights represent some of the most robust tools available to prevent ecological crisis'; and secondly, 'that the ways of life that Indigenous groups are protecting have a great deal to teach about how to relate to the land in ways that are not purely extractive'.[8] She also acknowledges the objectionable choices that impoverished Indigenous people often must make between their own economic survival and the survival of their land and ways of life. Deals offered by members of extractive industries may seem the best of the bad options. Tangible economic alternatives may not be available.

Conversely, Klein is very critical of those parts of the conservation and environmental movement that have drawn on a neoliberal capitalist logic of deregulation and privatisation to pursue their aims – those who have linked saving the planet to exciting new money-making opportunities. She argues that such claims involve intoxicating narratives, or magical thinking, which:

> assures us that however bad things get we're going to be saved – at the last minute – by the market, by philanthropist billionaires, or by technological Wizards.[9]

Klein writes:

> The idea that capitalism and only capitalism can save the
> world from a crisis created by capitalism is no longer an
> abstract theory; it's a hypothesis that has been tested and
> retested in the real world.[10]

In discussing those who have failed the tests, she examines the:

> venture capitalists who were supposed to bankroll a parade
> of innovation but they've come up far short: at the fraud
> invested boom and bust carbon market that has failed
> miserably to lower emissions: at the natural gas sector that
> was supposed to be our bridge to renewables but ended up
> devouring much of their market instead. And most of all,
> at the parade of billionaires who were going to invent a
> new form of enlightened capitalism but decided, on second
> thought, the old one was just too profitable to surrender.[11]

Klein's book, *The Shock Doctrine: The Rise of Disaster Capitalism*,[12] explains that capitalism seeks 'innovative' ways to profit from disaster. Disasters are coopted and become an exercise in social engineering: habituated community attitudes and sensibilities about social 'basics', such as the need for safety and the need to reduce heightened levels of anxiety, are mobilised and manipulated to extract support, approval and financial gain. At such times, conventional options melt away, and high-risk behaviours seem temporarily acceptable.

Climate change is clearly a global disaster that speaks 'in the language of fires, floods, droughts and extinctions'.[13] If shock doctrine principles are applied, even more disasters will undoubtedly follow. However, in *This Changes Everything*, Klein considers the possibility of an 'inverted shock doctrine' which does not involve exploiting the crises but, rather, involves seeking ways to address the many underlying problems that have led to it:

> There is no reason why future disasters cannot be
> laboratories for those who believe in reviving and

reinventing the Commons and in ways that actively reduce the chances that we will all be battered by many more such devastating blows in the future.[14]

Tony Birch is a highly acclaimed Australian fiction writer. He is also an academic and activist who writes and speaks on many platforms about issues associated with Indigenous history and knowledge, climate change and climate justice. I draw on his various published articles, chapters and speeches but note that there is often a close relationship between his fiction, his academic work and his activism. While his focus is usually on Australia, he makes connections to work with similar foci worldwide.

Birch challenges many dominant versions of Australian history. He highlights the ongoing history of settler colonialism in this country, particularly agricultural and industrial expansion, and draws out the implications for Indigenous people and their land. This expansion involved, and continues to involve, the dispossession, appropriation and exploitation of Indigenous land – ultimately, to extract economic value. Justifying this violent process, Birch argues, was 'a fabricated narrative of Indigenous savagery and civil absence, a narrative that legitimated theft of land and destruction of people'.[15] An accompanying narrative was *terra nullius*, the myth of an untouched land ready and primed for occupation. Indigenous people had no presence. The effects on Indigenous people were, and continue to be, profound, obliterating Indigenous sovereignty and ownership of country. In severing their connection to their land, settler colonialism also denied their culture, knowledge and spirit.

Birch also points to the co-dependent relationship between colonialism and capitalism. He insists that capitalism necessitates both environmental destruction and the destruction of whatever and whoever gets in its way:

Historically those who have been the most forceful barrier to an exploitative capitalist extraction mentality have been Indigenous nations, who, because of their acts of sovereignty and self-determination, have suffered levels of violence and dispossession beyond that experienced by other vulnerable and exploited communities.[16]

Mining is clearly implicated in all of this. Birch focuses on three main issues. The first is the connections concocted between the extraction of value from the land and Australia's nation-building projects. Secondly, he points to the longstanding ties between mining and the State:

> the mining industry has been a major beneficiary of government policy and legislation framed to ensure that the exploitation of land proceeds unhindered, with companies taking advantage of privileges ranging from generous tax subsidies to the granting of mining leases that disqualify Indigenous peoples' ability to access country.[17]

Along with this came administrative systems developed to count, record and 'manage' Indigenous people – to watch, control and corral them and to restrict and direct their movements. Colonial governments introduced various pieces of legislation, including Protection Acts.

Thirdly, Birch identifies the problems that arise now that Native Title is part of government legislation and land rights part of public discourse. Indigenous people must grapple with very difficult legal processes and very restricted readings of both; in effect:

> If a mining venture is opposed by Indigenous people, but supported by government, mining takes precedent over Indigenous property rights, even when land is 'protected' by the Native Title Act 1993 – Cwlth.[18]

Further, Birch explains that land rights are not the same as Native Title. Land rights are about the rights of the land itself – the land as an entity.

Birch makes the point that Indigenous communities also have highly uneven relationships with the companies that mine fossil fuels. They are faced with invidious 'choices' – to allow

mining to go ahead on their land and to try to negotiate a beneficial settlement or to refuse in order to protect their land, culture
and the planet.[19] He calls their dilemma 'Cash over Country'.

These negotiations are about such things as royalties,
jobs, training, education, health, housing and basic services.
Indigenous people's needs are considerable in all these areas.
Almost invariably, the negotiations are terribly imbalanced, and
the outcomes for Indigenous people are less than favourable.

Bitter tensions can arise within Indigenous communities
about whether to negotiate or to refuse. Whatever the case, on
the bigger stage, mining companies present themselves as either benevolent benefactors or as hapless victims of Indigenous
people's intransigence, standing in the way of progress.

Again, the State may come into play to 'broker' the relationships between Indigenous people and mining companies. It
often legislates in favour of mining companies on such things
as the deregistration of sacred sites and even the extinguish-
ment of Native Title. Under current Native Title legislation,
Indigenous communities do not have rights of veto. In response,
reform focused politics should work on permanently securing
basic rights, including appropriate forms of work, education
and health care, as well decent royalty payments.

Birch also addresses climate change, climate justice and the
ways that Indigenous people are caught up in both. He argues
that Indigenous people have experienced the greatest impact
of climate change, because it is a direct threat to their country,
culture and identity. He makes the case that they hold the keys
to addressing it:

> Decolonised ways of thinking and acting are vitally
> necessary if country is to be valued not as a saleable
> commodity or an exploited symbol of national pride but
> as an autonomous entity that each of us is connected to
> but does not own. 'Land Rights' is not simply a political
> catchcry or the basis of a legitimate and important
> political struggle. In relation to acting on climate change
> we must engage with the idea of the inherent rights of
> land, including the right to reciprocity, recompense for

past damages and a future of healing as a vital tenet of climate justice.[20]

Klein and Birch have been important guides on my educational journey, compelling me to think differently and deeply about the mining sites I visited and the liminal spaces I travelled through. They have helped free me from the 'commonsense' ideas I grew up with and the mining and tourist dogmas that continue to dominate the ideological landscape. In exposing the links between mining and the formidable troika of capitalism, colonialism and the State, Klein and Birch have clarified the power dynamics involved in the worlds of mining. In the following pages, I put their ideas to work and illustrate how this troika thrives on extractivism. I show how, in each place, it appropriates and commodifies nature; treats workers as useful but disposable; and regards other local humans as either convenient or irrelevant. I will demonstrate how these locations and the spaces between them are mining's sacrifice zones. Indigenous people have been forced to sacrifice the most. The notion of *terra nullius* is central to mining's extractivism and to the State's use of Indigenous land, which it appropriates for whatever nefarious purposes it chooses. Klein and Birch call for narratives about mining that identify the problems it creates. I offer stories about how such problems are experienced in the everyday life of place. I also turn to Indigenous people's storylines about their relationship to the land. From these, I learn that they are the land's original and best stewards.

PART THREE

Mining Localities, Dislocated Communities

5.
Poisonous Legacies: Broken Hill

Land of the Wilyakali language group

Overview

Broken Hill is located 850 km north-west of Melbourne, 1,100 km west of Sydney, 500 km north-east of Adelaide. The city is close to the convergence point of the borders of SA, NSW and Victoria. More specifically known as the Darling River Basin, this region is the traditional home of the Wilyakali people.

During the early days of the colonial period, it was a pastoral zone. Subsequently, fame and fortune came from the geological structures of the adjacent Barrier Ranges. In 1883, a pastoral worker named Charles Rasp noticed what he believed to be signs of tin deposits. With six others, Rasp formed the Syndicate of Seven and secured a series of mining leases that became BHP on 13 August 1885. The company quickly emerged as a mining powerhouse, expanding the scope of its operations, employing a growing workforce and generating significant financial returns to shareholders. By 1890, it was paying £1 million in dividends.

The ore body was a vast deposit of lead–silver–zinc, dubbed the Line of Lode. It is reputed to be one of the richest mineral deposits ever found and has produced over 300 million metric tonnes of ore. This discovery was the catalyst for the development of Broken Hill as a mining centre. By 1888, the town had a population of 11,000, growing to a peak of 35,000 in 1915, making it NSW's second largest municipality. The number of employees also grew dramatically, peaking at approximately 8,800 in 1907. Mining still occurs in Broken Hill, making it one of the longest lasting mining sites in the world. In the 2021 census, Broken Hill's population was 17,588, with a median age of 44 years and an Aboriginal and/or Torres Strait Islander population of 1,751.

I chose Broken Hill as the first site to visit because of its status as one of the most important mining locations in the country. Broken Hill is not only famous as the site of a rich deposit of silver, lead and zinc, returning ore valued in the billions of dollars; it was also a key location in the long chain of developments associated with Australia's industrialisation in the early 20th century. Important innovations in modern mining were developed there, including the 'flotation' method. It is also the birthplace of the global mega corporation BHP. It has a rich heritage of trade unionism, including strikes in 1892, 1909 and 1919; the 1919 conflict lasted for 18 months, ending with agreement to the 35-hour working week.

More recently, Broken Hill has become a location for the filming of some of Australia's most successful and iconic movies: *Wake in Fright* (1971), *A Town Like Alice* (TV miniseries, 1981), *A Place to Call Home* (1987), *Mad Max II* (1981), *Flying Doctors* (TV series, 1986–1992), *Reckless Kelly* (1993), *The Adventures of Priscilla, Queen of the Desert* (1994), *The Missing* (1998), *Mission Impossible II* (2000) and *RFDS: Royal Flying Doctor Service* (TV, 2021).

Broken Hill and nearby Silverton have also been the locations for the filming of countless commercials, giving many people a superficial understanding of the nature of this location as a key gateway to Australia's literal and mythical 'outback'. Before my visit I had little understanding of the location's rich history of industrial conflict.

Strike city

1892: the 16 weeks strike

Christine Adams' 'The Silver City: A Medical History' begins: 'The pioneers of Broken Hill and surrounding areas were, by necessity, tough and hardy'.[1] Conditions were certainly difficult.

One major factor affecting community health and wellbeing was access to a safe and secure water supply. As the population of the community expanded in line with the opportunities for work in the mines, the strains on the existing, inadequate water supplies became extreme. Subsequent outbreaks of typhoid resulted, including one in 1888 that killed 128 people.

Lead poisoning was another issue; the danger of lead-infused dust in the air was not well understood. One source was large piles of excavated dirt accumulating around the edges of mine sites, especially during bouts of windy weather. For the miners working underground, the enclosed quarters of the shafts became exposure sites for the inhalation of contaminated dust. Pneumoconiosis – black lung disease – became an occupational health problem.

In May 1892, the Barrier Ranges Mining Managers Association (MMA) moved to terminate some work conditions that had been formalised in 1889–90. Miners struck immediately, setting up picket lines. The MMA put in place arrangements to open the mine sites to non-union labour and gained state support, in the form of extra police in the city. Inevitably, violent confrontations followed, and several key mining officials were arrested. When strike officials announced the end of the strike, on 8 November 1892, the MMA had secured the use of contract labour, a 10 percent decrease in wages and a return to a 48-hour working week. The strike leaders lost support, and union membership plummeted.

Women, however, had been mobilised. They emerged from this struggle as political agents who, individually and collectively, could be an influential force in the streets, on the frontline in confrontations and within the picket line brigades.

1909: the lockout

Again in 1909, the owners and managers precipitated the conflict, claiming that wages must be reduced. BHP, rapidly becoming the big industrial thug, upped the ante: leaders announced that they would coordinate workplace lockouts for miners who were not prepared to accept a reduction in wages.

In late 1908, in anticipation of the 31 December end to a signed agreement, union leaders recruited Tom Mann, a highly credentialed activist and organiser. He arrived in Broken Hill in late September and immediately met with key union officials and leaders of groups. Three weeks after arriving in Broken Hill, he had recruited an estimated 1,600 miners into the unions. He also visited Port Pirie (SA), where many of the same industrial inequities and health problems existed because of excessive lead levels in the environment and emissions from the smokestacks.

During this hiatus period, leading up to the end of the agreement period and the start of the inevitable confrontation, the *Barrier Daily Truth*, established in 1898 as Broken Hill's local newspaper, became a daily paper. The Barrier Industrial Council owns it, and it is one of the few remaining independent newspapers in Australia.

As they had done back in 1892, the owners and their operatives had prepared for union pushback by lobbying to have extra police sent to Broken Hill. One police contingent arrived in November 1908 and two more in early January 1909. Under Mann's leadership, the unionists set up picket lines in three eight-hour shifts, providing 24-hour frontline security. Importantly, changeovers were reinforced by large numbers of union supporters, assembled behind the front row, including large numbers of women and a contingent of young girls at the rear.

On 9 January 1909, during the afternoon picket line changeover, a line of police blocked a very large group of marchers and directed them into a side street. This was an ambush. Tom Mann was seized, arrested and taken away, along with many unionists. Mann was bailed on condition that he did not participate in political activity. Police court proceedings began in late January but were then delayed. The trials were eventually conducted in Albury, far from Broken Hill, in May 1909. There were five charges against Mann, including sedition and unlawful assembly. In the trial by jury, he was acquitted. Mann left Broken Hill in June, and Percy Laidler replaced him.

Laidler was an effective organiser of unemployed workers.

Using syndicalist logics and methods, he focused on the development of locally based union organisations. He was also politically advanced in his use of emergent media technologies. He provoked political responses from conservatives through speeches and pamphlets that were then condensed and shared via telegrams. He advocated extreme measures and tactics designed to gain attention. A prime example was when he promoted the idea of unemployed miners taking over Broken Hill's British Mine. His motive in upping the ante in this way was to provoke the NSW Government into providing unemployment support. The effectiveness of this attention seeking method is evident in the tone and the content of a cable sent by Charles Wade, Premier of NSW, to Jack Long, Mayor of Broken Hill during the 1909 Lockout:

> Your wire received. Representation will be placed before
> cabinet and answer will be given possibly on Monday. In
> the meantime, I would urge you as head of municipality of
> Broken Hill to use effort to check wild language that is being
> indulged in.[2]

Mann and Laidler's orchestrated campaigns attracted financial support for miners from many different sources: local, interstate and overseas. Bill O'Neil, a member of three generations of Broken Hill miners, recorded some details of donations:

> In the 1909 dispute, various unions contributed £14,798
> through levies on workers in the Broken Hill region.
> Unions and individuals as far away as WA and New
> Zealand donated another £30,658. The London Dockers,
> who had received funds for the fight for the 'Dockers
> tanner' in 1892, helped too. The proceeds covered legal
> fees and sustained workers and families with Union Store
> coupons in various denominations (from seven shillings,
> six pence up to 20 shillings) and bread coupons for the
> duration of the strike.[3]

1915–1916 Disputes

Subsequent stoppages secured some significant gains. In June 1916, the Federal Arbitration Court, presided over by Justice Higgins, introduced a ruling of a 44-hour week for underground miners, a 48-hour week for above-ground workers and an increase in wages. The role played by Higgins in these judgements is worth some attention, because it involves a legal precedent that created a clear division between the needs of workers and profit-driven motives and practices of owners.

The Harvester Case

In 1907, Justice Higgins had presided over a case involving H. V. McKay, employer and owner of a factory producing agricultural machinery. To avoid paying an excise duty, McKay had to establish that he paid his workers a fair and reasonable wage. He attempted to do this through the newly created Commonwealth Court of Conciliation and Arbitration. This subsequently became known as the Harvester Case.

While reaching his conclusion and making a judgement about McKay's claim, Higgins took great care in investigating the concept of a 'fair and reasonable wage'. He quickly discovered that there was no legally established ruling. Accordingly, he set about creating an outcome that would then become a legal benchmark. Higgins' subsequent ruling had important implications for Australian labour law.

At the centre of Higgins' judgement was a premise that fair and reasonable wages for unskilled workers were sufficient for a human being in a civilised community to support self and dependants in frugal comfort, and for skilled workers to gain higher wages in recognition of the productive value of their skills. What emerged in labour law was the concept of a basic or minimum wage.

In an exchange that describes the logic and ethics that he applied in making his ruling, Higgins also made clear assumptions about what he believed constituted a decent minimum wage for workers. He stated:

> In the Harvester Case, I had to find what was 'fair and
> reasonable remuneration' for certain classes of employees.
> I considered that no remuneration could be treated as fair
> and reasonable which did not, at the least, allow for the
> satisfaction of the 'normal wants of an average employee
> regarded as a human being living in a civilised community'.
> Among the normal wants, I include food, shelter, clothing
> – and family life. This family life cannot be had, under
> existing conditions, without money wherewith to maintain
> a wife and children. I do not take the family as the unit as
> you think. I take the employee as the unit, with normal
> wants. The principle which I adopted in the Harvester Case
> I have applied in my awards; for in awards, for settling
> disputes, the essential condition of peace is that the
> employee receive a fair and reasonable remuneration. I do
> not say anything with regard to the merits or faults of large
> schemes for social betterment.[4]

Higgins' ruling created a benchmark for Conciliation and
Arbitration that has reverberated down through court rulings
to present times. While obviously narrow, limited and gender
blind, his judgement mechanism recognised the basic needs
and rights of workers.

Conscription

Later in 1916, Broken Hill miners became embroiled in wartime politics in the fight against military conscription. From the
outset of Australian involvement in WW1 battles in Europe, the
government increased demands on, and control over, mining at
Broken Hill. At stake was a large supply of lead, to be used in the
production of munitions. In response, a cadre of miners formed
the Labor Volunteer Army and pledged to campaign against
conscription and to protect the independence of unions.

1919–1920: the Big Strike

In June 1997, the NSW Parliament's Legislative Council provided an account of 'Broken Hill Trade Unionism'. During his report, Mark Kersten provided an account of what became known
as the Big Strike, a dispute that lasted 18 months. His statement
provides a useful introductory description:

> The next great struggle of the union movement in Broken
> Hill was the famous strike of 1919–20, which was fought over
> safety conditions in the mines and eventually resulted in the
> Holman Labor Government setting up a royal commission
> into the mining industry at Broken Hill.[5]

In her article, 'Broken Hill: A radical history', Sandra
Bloodworth takes up the story:

> More than one historian has described it as the biggest
> industrial battle in Australian history. Thousands were on
> strike from May 1919 to November 1920. These 18 months
> brought hardship, sacrifice and near starvation but could
> not erode their traditions of solidarity and determination.[6]

Bloodworth captures the challenges of illness and desper-
ation and highlights the significant gains achieved through
solidarity – forged from a combination of collective struggle
within a tight-knit and isolated community and from clever
union leadership.

Kersten's assertion that the strike was basically a struggle
over work conditions is key to making sense of the protracted
event of 1919–20. A crucial element here is the impact on the
health of miners and their families of lead infusions in the air,
soil and water.

Journalist Craig Brealey provides a useful summary of key
findings of a commission of inquiry and an independent tribu-
nal, led by Justice Edmunds, into the health of miners:
* Two thousand underground workers were examined.
* Of those, 251 were found too ill to work in the mines
  any more.

- Twenty-five of them died during the inquiry.
- Almost 40 men were found to have chronic lead poisoning.

In September 1920, Edmunds presented his final decision:

- The 35-hour week – five shifts, seven hours a day – was granted to underground workers.
- Firing was to be carried out during an hour's break between shifts, so the dust could settle.
- Night stoping was abolished.
- The 'two men to one machine' rule was introduced for safety and to allow one worker to spray water on the drilling site to reduce dust.
- A minimum wage of 15 shillings a day was awarded, and overtime was to be paid at time-and-a-half during the week and double-time on the Sunday shift.
- Employees who were injured on the job and had to leave work were also to be paid for the whole shift, and time lost was to be paid by the mines.
- Workers suffering from occupation diseases were awarded compensation of two pounds a week plus an extra one pound, 17 shillings for their dependants.

Negotiations continued, and the mines and unions eventually agreed to a settlement.

The Big Strike started in 1919 and lasted for 18 months. The battle against BHP, the other companies and the NSW Government ended in victory for the Broken Hill unions in November 1920. They won safer working conditions underground, better pay and compensation for widows and injured miners.

This short history transports us back to the earliest years of mining at Broken Hill when miners, mine owners and their managers were involved in several production-shaping disputes. Leaders, including Mann and Laidler, established the groundwork for effective collective action. The strikes are an important part of the history of Australia's industrial relations.

My visit

My drive to Broken Hill from Melbourne stretched over two days, broken by an overnight stay in Mildura. After crossing the Murray River at Mildura and then the Darling River at Wentworth, I drove north for approximately 250 km. The country is flat, the highway long and straight, the sky cloudless. The vegetation along this expanse of flat plains is a mix of saltbush, bluebush, small mallee eucalyptus and some stands of casuarina. Although I didn't realise it at the time, this was to be my entry into many days of travel through similar terrain. Feral horses and goats feeding alongside the highway provided an unofficial welcome to Broken Hill.

The city is divided into two main sections by what appeared to be a large mullock hill made up of overburden from the mining process. I later realised that this 'hill' was the remnants of the incredibly wealth-generating Line of Lode deposit of ore.

To the north of this dividing ridge is the city central; to the south is a smaller suburb of South Broken Hill. Two buildings perched atop the hill caught my eye: the Line of Lode Miners Memorial structure and the Visitor Information Centre, two distinctive landmarks in the northern side of the city.

In many ways, the story of the changing fortunes and challenges of this remotely located city is evident in the architecture. Alongside a host of heritage-listed buildings, symbolising the prosperity and aspirations of the early boom years of 1890–1920, are humble miners' cottages constructed of corrugated iron. In the absence of readily available building materials, because of the city's arid location, it was cheaper and more efficient to build houses from iron transported from the coastal cities. I can imagine how uncomfortable these houses must have been in times of extreme heat and cold.

Features of the main part of the city, to the north of the hill, include the city shopping precinct, the administrative centre for the region, the famous Trades Hall Council building and an expansive cemetery. I spent the better part of my first day and a half walking around these different locations, drilling down into old records in the public library and visiting the Visitors

Line of Lode Memorial to miners who have died, Broken Hill, NSW

Centre and Line of Lode Miners Memorial perched on top of the hill. The memorial offers an excellent overview of the northern side of the city and the countryside beyond, but it is a sobering place to visit. It records the names of over 800 miners who died because of mining accidents or disease. I noticed a significant number of plaques attributing the cause of death to 'lead poisoning'. In 1929, the start of the Great Depression, there were five such inscriptions.

There are several houses in South Broken Hill adjacent to the operational Consolidated Broken Hill mining lease, and one or two butt up against the mullock heaps on the boundary line of the lease.

I parked and began my walk through the area. It was a few minutes before 9 am, and cars dropping off kids at the adjacent primary school created a buzz in the streets. Buses arrived in convoy to deliver their passengers to the school gate. Two

House and mine overburden in South
Broken Hill, NSW

boys casually made their way along the street and towards to the gate, chatting as one hopped on and off a skateboard while the other bounced a football. There was obviously no urgency about reaching and entering the school's gate. Their relaxed attitude amused me – they appeared to be totally aware of the time and were deliberately delaying their entry into the controlled world of the schoolyard. My hunch is that, given half a chance, they would have stayed in the street skating and kicking the hours away.

With my observations and photo shoot complete, I took one last drive around that part of the city. Some of the houses appeared so run down and unkempt that I wondered whether anyone was living there; I did feel some middle-class guilt for scrutinising and judging these places. My mind wandered back to the towns of the central Latrobe Valley in Victoria and the areas that looked similar. I know that those areas provide ultra-cheap housing and have thus attracted people, down on their luck, from the cities. I wondered whether it's the same situation here. I concluded that this part of Broken Hill would be a hard place to live, especially during a long, hot summer with a hot north wind pluming dust and dirt over the small suburb.

Issues

Dust, disease and painful memories

Deep inside the common narrative of industrial growth at Broken Hill, a different story has unfolded and is memorialised. Miners experienced serious industrial illnesses and continued to do so over time. Dust laden with lead was the culprit. Bunny Dwyer, who worked in the mines, provides a powerful testimony about the dangers and mental stress this situation created:

> There'd be three shifts, and…you'd be coming out the cage
> when your mates are going in. You'd have to shake hands,
> you couldn't see – the dust and smoke and everything…
> When you get in that cage, you never know when you're

coming up…you come up, but you might be dead or cut to pieces… Your life was a gamble.[7]

Patrick Francis Dwyer was born 25 March 1902 and began work at 12 years of age in 1914. He earned three shillings and sixpence for each day he could get work. Dwyer worked in the mines at Broken Hill until after World War II. He had ample reason to be circumspect about the dangers of mining for employees: he survived a 20-metre fall in 1934 and was present during mishaps that resulted in deaths and injuries of workmates.

Relatively recently, an annual memorial ceremony has been held on the Sunday closest to 8 October. This is the anniversary of the deaths of two young mullockers, Leopold Campbell, 21, and Thomas Jordan, 19, who were killed in a rock fall on 8 October 1902. Their bodies have never been recovered.

This memorial ceremony has evolved into a small-scale, sombre and simple event. Participants are encouraged to provide their own deck chairs. The service includes short speeches by local dignitaries and a minute's silence to honour those who have died because of mining at that location. The event went online in 2021 because of COVID-19 restrictions. Speaking about this change of format, the Deputy Mayor, Christine Adams, observed the benefit of online communication, including providing access to:

> thousands of ex-locals who have lost a family member or friend on the mines over the years…bringing the event to them…no matter where they are in the world.

At the 2020 ceremony, several important and related issues were raised. Greg Braes, Vice-president of the Construction, Forestry, Mining and Energy Union (CFMEU) in Broken Hill, observed that many more miners had died because of work-related illness resulting from dust and lead poisoning. Reverend Helen Ferguson and Mayor Darriea Turley reinforced and extended this point, acknowledging the toll taken on the lives of women and children who lived 'in horrific conditions' adjacent to the city's mines.[8]

The health/education legacy

Two months after my visit, an article about school test results caught my attention. My thoughts went back to the two boys casually wandering through the streets of Broken Hill South on their way to school.[9] Here is an excerpt from that article, 'Australia's most dangerous streets revealed by school testing':

> Accidents, illness, strangers: danger to children takes many forms. But for brain damage caused by toxic mining metals, the streets closest to the mines in Broken Hill, Mount Isa and Port Pirie must rank as the most dangerous in Australia. Children in these mining and smelting cities exposed to high levels of lead, arsenic and cadmium are more than twice as likely to have developmental delays than the national average, research shows.[10]

It reports the first research to link NAPLAN results to school catchment areas that are known to have high levels of toxic metals in the environment. It compared them with those of their peers around the country. The researchers found that children who lived closest to the lead and zinc mine in Broken Hill, where the exposure to toxic air, dust and soils were at their highest, had the consistently lowest literacy and numeracy scores in Years 3 and 5.

In a further article, the same researchers amplify the problems of the lead smelting legacy and the associated dangers for children:

> In the shadows of Broken Hill's rich mining history lies a legacy of contamination and regulatory failure that will likely outlive any benefits locals derive from mining.
>
> One in five children aged under five in Broken Hill have blood lead levels above the current national goal of ten micrograms per decilitre. And the trend is headed in the wrong direction.

Our research, published today in the journal *Environmental Research*, shows children are exposed to contaminants in play areas. Metal-rich dust accumulates continually on play surfaces and is readily picked up on the hands of children as they play. When they touch their mouth, they ingest the metal particles.[11]

The scope of this lead poisoning public health issue is well documented. It is a problem with a long legacy. It was identified in the early days of the smelting process, but the impact of lead poisoning on young children was recognised as a public health problem at the end of the 19th century and at the very beginning of large-scale production. The following excerpt illustrates the outcomes: 'In the town, mortality rate amongst children was extremely high. Fifty percent of deaths recorded in 1895 were children under the age of ten.'[12]

When the Broken Hill mines first opened in the 1880s, the ore was mainly lead carbonate (cerussite), an easily digested lead compound. This was refined in a series of smelters along the mine ridge, the highest point in the town. On windy days, lead-rich dust from the smelters landed everywhere. It settled on the roofs and drained into drinking water tanks. Cattle, sheep and dairy cows ate grass covered in lead dust, which flowed into the food chain. Although the miners and smelter workers were most likely to be affected, the entire population of Broken Hill was susceptible to lead poisoning.

Watching those two boys ambling along the dusty streets on their way to school, I observed a behaviour pattern that is part and parcel of the childhood years for many kids. In Broken Hill, this behaviour clearly comes at a cost. The price has been long recognised and written off as a collateral cost of the production process. This by-product of the complex web of productive elements makes these streets of South Broken Hill dangerous for residents. Meanwhile, no doubt, the major stake-holders and owners of the mine, CBH Resources Limited, have the relative luxury of living in faraway places well removed from such problems.

Further, when Broken Hill's production processes are placed within the larger context of smelting and processing in Australia, an even more disturbing picture of environmental and health-related damage becomes visible. Port Pirie, now with a century-long history of smelting, shares with Broken Hill and Mount Isa test results in primary school children showing delayed learning capacities.[13]

Remote control and the loss of the local

Though the dangers for locals have endured, the flow of capital with its associated payoffs has become more dynamic. While initial funding for the Broken Hill leaseholders came from relatively local bases of capital, including Melbourne and Sydney, sources of funding have become increasingly globalised. A key component in this process is the flow of information, which helps to inform the market about production output and the relative status of commodities in the competitive marketplace. Information analysts have become increasingly important operatives for corporations in managing the market health of their resources. Equally, engineers and highly skilled geologists play significant roles in generating information needed to fine-tune production and, at the same, to inform the market. Increasingly, onsite data gathering tools and high-speed information systems enable these monitoring and assessment tasks to be conducted in the comfort of offices. This narrative about Broken Hill is not an anomaly: it is a prime example of one of the many contradictions of globalising capitalism.

With the advent of sophisticated data gathering methods, high-speed information links, rapid transport systems and powerful technologies for calculating the metrics of market trends, the global movement of commodities has grown exponentially; for example, the market for fresh flowers in Europe is sustained by flowers grown in Africa. This demand in one place comes at a cost in other places. The rose industry of the Lake Naivasha (Kenya) region has created significant environmental damage and social conflict, because the lake's water supply is being drained to satisfy the production needs of a burgeoning number of growers. When the production process becomes unsustainable, commercial adjustments will see the industry switch to new locations, leaving behind a damaged environment that burdens those living locally.

BHP, the original owner of the big mine atop the 'broken hill', began to wind back its investments in ore mining as early as the second decade of the 20th century. The company's directors looked further afield and into the future, deciding that steelmaking was a viable growth area. BHP thus ceased its operations at Broken Hill in 1939. Currently, CBH Resources Limited owns the mine. The company's webpage summarises its Broken Hill operations:

> CBH Resources Limited is a significant producer of silver, lead and zinc in Australia... The Rasp Mine (Zn-Pb-Ag) at Broken Hill received development approval from the NSW government in January 2011 and construction was completed on schedule in April 2012. The Mine processes 700,000 tonnes of ore per annum to produce 28,000 tonnes of zinc metal in concentrate, 18,000 tonnes of lead metal and 1 million ounces of silver in the lead concentrate. Rasp Mine employs 200 people... Following a takeover in late 2010, CBH Resources Limited became a wholly owned subsidiary of Toho Zinc Co., Ltd, a Japanese company listed on the Tokyo Stock Exchange specializing in nonferrous metals refining.[14]

Perilya, a Perth-based company, also mines in Broken Hill. Perilya was established in 1987, with the aim of acquiring undervalued assets, purchasing the mine from Pasminco Limited. Perilya's prospectus refers to production at the mine:

> Due to the challenging economic environment at the time, the Company's operation at the Broken Hill mine went through a resizing in 2008, which has resulted in significant improvement in productivity, profitability and cash flow resulting in an extension to the life of the mine to approximately 10 years.[15]

Zhongin Lingnan Mining (HK) Company Limited, a Chinese company based in Shenzhen and involved in mining and processing nonferrous metals, including lead and zinc, took over Perilya in December 2013.

As ownership and control of the mining sites bounces around globally, working communities in Broken Hill continue to live within an environment laced with the long-term fallout of lead and other production by-products. But their capacity to influence their local circumstances has dramatically diminished.

6.
Pillaging water: Roxby Downs (SA)

Land of the Kokatha language group

Overview

The mining settlement of Roxby Downs and the Olympic Dam mine are 550 kms north-west of Adelaide in a very arid region of SA. Technically and geographically, they are positioned in the Tirari Desert. Many bores within the region extract water from the underground Great Artesian Basin. In the 2021 census, Roxby Downs' population was 3,976, with a median age of 31 and an Aboriginal and/or Torres Strait Islander population of 198.

Originally a remote cattle/sheep station, the site was marked for development in the mid-1970s following the discovery of a large mineral deposit. During the mid-1980s, the Western Mining Corporation and the SA Government entered a joint venture to develop a mine, with the town of Roxby Downs built to house employees. The joint venture officially opened in November 1988. Unlike many other mines, it is a fully integrated production site involving extraction processing, smelting and refining, all occurring in the one location. Such integration has resulted in tightly orchestrated management arrangements.

In 2005, BHP Billiton took control of the venture and almost immediately began to extend operations to create one of the world's largest mines, producing gold, silver, copper and uranium oxide and classed as a poly-metallic extraction site.

Over the following decade, several extensive initiatives were implemented, leading to a partial shutdown in operations in late 2017 while upgrades occurred. In February 2018, Olympic Dam Asset President Jacqui McGill, in tandem with SA's Premier Jay Weatherill and senior ministers, announced a further $350 million investment in the mine. McGill's speech highlighted the ongoing collaboration between the state and the company – an arrangement that was deemed to be important in 'increasing the global competitiveness of Olympic Dam through continuous improvements to our infrastructure, technology, and processes'.[1]

My visit

I arrived at Port Augusta after a trip that took just over four hours and covered 400 km. As I slowed to take the road to the Motor Inn, I noticed a large road sign ahead on the highway I was leaving. A white line on the right and branching off the A1 Highway was marked simply 'A87, Darwin, Northern Territory'. The white line branching to the left was marked 'A1, Eyre Highway, Perth, Western Australia'. This was the junction point of roads that traverse over half the continent.

The next day, I took the A87 north to Pimba and then Route B97. On the way, I made a small detour into Woomera, where I stopped to wander and look at the displays on notice boards about the story of the region's 'rocket range and testing ground'. Australia and the UK used a vast area of 122,188 square km as a long-range testing facility from 1947 through to the late 1970s. Media attention given to the site during the peak years of the Cold War and through into the 1990s must have been tightly controlled, but it did not occur to me that the site I was about to visit would also be tightly controlled.

I next drove through a long stretch of gibber plain containing very little vegetation. The country became more arid as I travelled further north on the B97. At one point, I stopped to take a photo of a single tree in a large expanse of stony ground and asked myself, 'Is this what they meant by *terra nullius*?'

The photo retains symbolic and political significance. It registers the reasons for my curiosity and suspicion when, a short time later, I drove into Roxby Downs and found something of an oasis. I immediately wondered about water: 'How can there be such a difference? Where does the water come from that produces the growth of large healthy trees and sustains a lush covering of grass over the football oval?'

I stayed in the only motel in town – expensive, because of its absolute monopoly. In a quick trip to the adjacent shopping centre, I discovered that mine tours are only offered on one day per week – the day I had arrived. If I wanted to look inside and underground at the Olympic Dam site, I would have to wait another week. I didn't have time to do that. Fortunately, I happened to meet a very helpful person at the Community Centre who promised that he would arrange a next-day screening of two documentary films about BHP Billiton's Olympic Dam above and below ground operations. I thanked him and walked away, feeling a mix of relief, satisfaction and good luck.

My sleep was fitful – disturbed by frustration and self-doubt about what I was attempting on this trip. After having had such a productive and inspiring time in Broken Hill, I struggled with the thought that I should have selected my target sites with greater care and better preparation. At 6 am, I decided to take an early morning walk. I recognised that my visit to this place would not necessarily yield as much as I had hoped, but I had to make the most of the situation. I walked into the town of Roxby Downs.

It is a company town, highly ordered and regulated, designed to cater for workers at the Olympic Dam mine at a rather minimal level. The houses were all single storey and air conditioned, with three or four bedrooms and exteriors of pale cladding or brick veneer. The grounds were barren and dotted with scrubby plants suited to the extreme weather conditions – despite the readily available bore water. Most driveways held the standard 4WD. The unkempt gardens suggest that the workers do not plan to stay long, and the cross-country vehicle at the ready suggests a need to regularly escape. Much later, after my visit, I discovered that the local cemetery is empty – apart from weeds and a few feral animals. People who die in Roxby Downs are taken and buried in locations elsewhere. The empty cemetery signifies the transient nature of Roxby Downs' population. I infer from this

that Roxby Downs is not a place that people consider as their genuine home. Even the dead leave town.

At 8.45 am, I set off for a quick trip to the mine and the adjacent Olympic Dam Village. It was only a short distance. Because I already knew that I didn't have access to the mine site, my trip became a firsthand sighting of big signs barring entry to people without permits. That also applied to entry to the Village, where signs again stressed that there was no access unless visitors were employees or were on official business. Moreover, all cars permitted into the official carpark had to be reversed into the spaces – it was not clear why. Because it was very early morning, and nothing much was happening, I decided to ignore BHP Billiton's paramilitary organisation and park 'illegally' so that I could walk to a little hillock to get a photo of the worksite in the distance. I completed this mission without any drama.

I returned to Roxby Downs and headed to the Community Centre for my private screening. The staff member had generously arranged everything, and the film was set to start. I ordered my morning's obligatory flat white coffee, which the young woman serving offered to bring me in the mini theatre. Within minutes, I sat alone in the comfortable little venue absorbing myself in the slick BHP Billiton spin on the 'whys, hows and wherefores' of the Olympic Dam mine site.

The films provided a large amount of information, much of it in the abstract jargon of mineral exploration and extraction and different processing methods. The workers were an absent presence. I was struck by the contrast with the 'stories' of Broken Hill that I had recently explored. I thought of the visual power of the Line of Lode Miners Memorial perched on top of the broken hill as a tribute to the hundreds of miners who died because of their work.

Roxby Downs/Olympic Dam is, first and foremost, shaped in the image of 'the company'. It seemed designed to constantly reinforce the message that the owners/shareholders/investors matter most of all. The 'workforce' – in the most extended sense of individuals, families and community support systems – is just an appendage. Put slightly more generously, the workforce is a component of the production process that sits at the bottom end of the industrial/corporate hierarchy. Understood in these terms, Roxby Downs/Olympic Dam exists in sharp contrast with Broken Hill, where the achievements and relative importance of the miners, as a workforce, was celebrated and continues to be recognised as a signifier of workforce importance and collective achievement. At this site, here in Roxby Downs/Olympic Dam, the company, BHP Billiton, has its corporate stamp on everything and everyone.

One image caught my attention: a view of a huge water storage unit inside the mine site. My curiosity was primed; I knew there was more to discover about the sources of large amounts of water and a lush oasis in an arid part of the driest state of the driest continent on earth. Subsequently, in my post-trip research, I was able to turn my attention to this issue and to discover several significant details about what has made this access to large quantities of water possible.

Issues

Corporate control and state capture

During my short visit, I quickly discovered the extent of the corporate control of movement into and through areas associated with the mining site proper. With limited public access to the mine site, the generation of firsthand information about the place is limited and filtered through BHP Billiton's public relations mechanism. This mechanism of corporate control has not occurred by chance: it is built into the legal and administrative framework that was put in place at the very beginning of the site's history.

When Australia first entered the era of neoliberal politics, the SA Government struck a deal with several mining companies to establish a joint mining venture. This arrangement was formally ratified in the *Roxby Downs (Indenture Ratification) Act 1982*, a legal arrangement that:

> ratifies a contract between the State of South Australia and a group of companies covering the construction, maintenance,

and operation of a mine in the Olympic Dam Area or another selected area and related facilities, in particular a treatment plant. The minerals to be worked include uranium.[2]

In practice, this Act and its subsequent amendments ratified a joint state–corporations venture in SA that is exempt from important environmental and Indigenous rights statutes. Significantly, a large part of the Act deals with matters of water access and use.

The Roxby Downs/Olympic Dam joint venture uses 35 million litres of Great Artesian Basin water per day. This is one of the more controversial aspects of the venture. Advocates, including academics who have been invited to write on behalf of key stakeholders, argue that water use is 'sustainable' and justified. Torrisi and Trotta assert:

> Most of the water to the Olympic Dam mine and the nearby
> townships of Roxby Downs and Andamooka is supplied from
> the Great Artesian Basin (GAB). There are no permanent
> local water sources available to Olympic Dam. The use
> of water from the Great Artesian Basin by Olympic Dam
> receives considerable attention by BHP Billiton and is
> extensively regulated by the Government of South Australia.
> Olympic Dam has robust business management systems
> in place to ensure the sustainable use of water from the
> GAB including ISO9001 and ISO14001 systems to deliver
> the targeted outcomes and obligations of the Olympic Dam
> Environmental Management and Monitoring Program. The
> management systems ensure that Olympic Dam retains
> accountability for its water demand from the GAB over the
> life of the mine.[3]

In contrast, Friends of the Earth Australia has challenged many of Torrisi and Trotta's assumptions in *Olympic Dam – Summary of Major Concerns*.[4] The Olympic Dam mine has been dubbed a state within a state, having been established by a specific act of State Parliament, the *Roxby Downs Indenture Act*. The Indenture Act allows Olympic Dam wide-ranging exemptions from environmental laws, water management laws and Aboriginal Heritage laws – and for good measure it curtails the application of the Freedom of Information Act. In this way workers have been blocked from providing specific information about production processes.

The exemptions from laws that are central to good mining management – environmental, water and Aboriginal Heritage – are shocking. It is no wonder that Olympic Dam ruthlessly polices its borders and its image. In Klein's terms, this place is a 'sacrifice zone'.

Water damage

The use of water in the mine's production processes interested me before I arrived at Roxby Downs and increased in importance as I examined it. This is a broad and complex issue:

> The Olympic Dam mine uses 35 million litres of Great Artesian Basin water each day, making it the largest industrial user of underground water in the southern hemisphere. Water is pumped along an underground pipeline from two bore fields which are located 110 km and 200 km to the north of the mine. The salty bore water requires desalination before it is used. Contaminated water from mining operations is passed through a series of sealed ponds where it evaporates. 3 megalitres of the 35 megalitres extracted daily is supplied to the township of Roxby Downs. Water usage has increased significantly since the 1990s. In 1995, the Olympic Dam project, including the Roxby Downs township, consumed an average of 14.3 megalitres of water daily.

> The high use of artesian water as a result of mine operations threatens areas of high ecological significance. In particular, the pumping of water from the bore fields has been linked to observations of reductions in flow or drying out in nearby mound springs. As mound springs are the only permanent source of water in the arid interior of South Australia, a

delicate yet intricate ecological balance has been established
with prolonged isolation causing the existence of many rare
and endemic species.[5]

Roxby Downs is an isolated, remote location in an extremely
arid environment. It is approximately 560 kms from Adelaide,
1,100 kms from Alice Springs and 1,800 kms from Sydney. The
Koppen and Geiger classification of climate rates it as BWh,
meaning arid and warm. The average annual temperature is
20.5°C, and yearly rainfall is 171 mm (6.7 in).[6] These details put
the prefabricated, company stamped and controlled appearance
into perspective.

In terms of keeping up appearances, water availability and use
is not an issue; but, in the bigger scheme of events, it is. The deal
to access water from the Great Artesian Basin involves a mutu-
ally beneficial financial arrangement between big business and
the state. The company is free to extract mineral-based wealth
and water from the ground, apparently in any manner it pleases.
And the SA Government gets some associated revenue in return.
This does not seem like a fair return for the state or its citizens.
But the problems don't stop there. This arrangement not only
lacks proper transparency and accountability; it fails to account
for widespread concerns about the future supply of water.

This chapter has highlighted two issues: uranium is mined at
Olympic Dam, and the mining process requires large quantities
of water. These developments are interconnected. Considering
growing concerns about global warming and associated climate
change, alternative energy sources are needed to replace atmospheric pollution caused by fossil fuels. Uranium as a fuel source
for atomic energy production is one alternative. Paradoxically,
the high use of water supplies in the arid environment of SA
dramatises a tension at the very heart of many mining practices. At what point do environmental changes offset the benefits
generated by alternatives to burning highly polluting fossil
fuels? Embedded within the question is the second issue: at
what point does a government, federal or state, cross the line of
public responsibility in dealing with the global climate crisis in
the effort to extract surplus wealth for the public coffers?

7.

Rough cuts: The Argyle diamond mine (WA)

Land of the Kija language group

Overview

The Argyle diamond mine is in the East Kimberley region in the far north of WA. The Kimberley is a large region of 423,517 square km with a population of 36,000. It is approximately the same size as Uzbekistan (population 28.66 million) and larger than New Zealand (268,021 sq km, population 4.89 million) and Japan (377,975.26 sq km, population 125.82 million). A large area with a small population, it has another equally significant feature. The combined effects of geographic remoteness and rich, diverse ecosystems generate varied reactions. Writer Tim Winton lauds the Kimberley as a 'remarkable and complex' region.[1] Geophysical diversity and remoteness combine to signify a unique region loaded with opportunities for sightseeing, creative inspiration and adventure – as well as economic development and exploitation. But diamond mining also involved many activities elsewhere. Diamonds mined in the Kimberley were initially processed, cut and polished in Perth, or in some cases India, and then marketed and sold in metropolitan and cosmopolitan locations in Australia, Europe, Asia and the USA.

When I left Melbourne in mid-July, I drove away from a cold maritime location at the extreme south-east of the continent. The stock of warm clothing I packed for the trip was evidence

Mt Whaleback iron ore mine, Newman, W.A.

of my winter mindset. By the time I drove out of the Northern Territory (NT) and into the extreme north-west of WA, I was in a totally different climate zone. Australia's Bureau of Meteorology climate statistics highlight this point: in Kununurra, the town that became my base for this part of the trip, the mean temperature for August is 33.6°C, the mean rainfall is 0.1 mm and the mean number of clear days per month is 22.7. I packed away my Melbourne winter clothing and bought clothing more suitable to this part of the world.

The region holds five major population centres: Broome (population 16,959) and Derby (3,322) in the south; Kununurra (7,477) in the north-east; and, centrally positioned, Halls Creek (3,574) and Fitzroy Crossing (1,181). The economy of the region involves a mix of tourism, mining, agriculture, Indigenous artwork and aquaculture. Climatically, the Kimberley has two seasons: 'the wet' (November–April) and 'the dry' (May–October). This division is reflected in average annual rainfall totals. Kununurra sees rainfall averaging between 213 mm (February) and 0.1 mm (August).[2]

The former Argyle diamond mine, once a fly-in fly-out (FIFO) destination for miners, lies in a valley south of Lake Argyle, approximately 180 km south of Kununurra and 246 km north of Halls Creek. Open pit mining began in December 1985. The diamonds were graded as relatively low quality, but the site produced large amounts of marketable stones, including a variety of natural-coloured diamonds.

Rio Tinto, a multinational corporation with its headquarters in London, mined diamonds in the East Kimberley. The company's website for the Argyle mine begins with a snapshot of key features about the site and its history:

East Kimberley, Western Australia

Our Argyle diamond mine became one of the world's largest producers of diamonds and the largest supplier of natural-coloured diamonds – including white, champagne, cognac, blue, violet and the rare and the highly-coveted Argyle pink and red diamonds.

In November 2020 mining ceased at Argyle, after 37 years of operations and producing more than 865 million carats of rough diamonds.

We are committed to respectfully closing and rehabilitating the mine and returning the land to its traditional custodians.

The technologically sophisticated underground operation at Argyle was the first block cave mine in Western Australia.

Argyle's direct contribution to the East Kimberley represents approximately 6 percent of the region's gross regional product – a relatively small, but still important, component of the local economy.

Argyle diamond mine is preparing for closure in late 2020…it will take three to five years to decommission and dismantle the mine and start rehabilitation followed by environmental monitoring and maintenance.

We are working closely with these stakeholders and government to gain input into closure planning and prepare for the transition beyond closure.[3]

In another industry communiqué, Rio Tinto advertised a collection of pink diamonds showcased for sale in New York, quoting then Vice-president Alan Chirgwin:

It is 40 years since the discovery of Rio Tinto's Argyle mine and it remains the first and only ongoing source of rare pink diamonds in the world, in history. With the lifecycle of this extraordinary mine approaching its end, we have seen and continue to see, an unstoppable demand and strong value appreciation for these truly limited-edition diamonds.[4]

The 2019 Argyle Pink Diamonds Tender collection, titled 'The Quest for the Absolute', comprises 'six hero diamonds named in honour of their mystical heritage and timeless embodiment of beauty'.[5]

Both statements contained several key selling points. On the world scene, the Argyle natural-coloured diamonds were rare and exclusive – intended only for the ultra-rich. To extract them required cutting-edge technology and mining knowhow. Conversely, the company acknowledged that the stones had been extracted from the land of traditional occupants. The implication was that its extraction of such precious minerals involved due acknowledgement of, and negotiated arrangements with, Indigenous landowners. As is so often the case, the realpolitik of the situation is much more complex and contradictory.

My visit

Early in the morning of 3 August, I left Kununurra and drove towards Derby, on the coast in the far south-west of the Kimberley. Given the distance, I didn't expect to be there until the next day. Part of my reasoning about the time the trip would take was based on my plans to take a side trip to visit the Argyle Diamond Mine, 180 km to the south.

Not far into this journey, I turned off the Victoria Highway and onto the Great Northern Highway (#95), a route that goes all the way to Perth, 3,000 km south. Just beyond this turn, I noticed a hitchhiker going my way. Stepping out of the shade of some trees as I approached, the hitchhiker used an unusual hitching gesture of holding out an open palm, as distinct from the age-old thumb in the air technique, to catch drivers' attention. This person was dressed for the heat: big floppy hat, long-sleeved shirt and long khaki pants. I noticed a small collection of bags back in the shade of the trees. I considered it for a moment but didn't stop. I needed to retain the flexibility to stop whenever I wanted, to take photos and study rock features in that area of the Kimberley. My timing for this section of the journey was excellent. The early morning sunlight was lighting up the east-facing rock faces and cliffs of the Durack Range. I had stopped numerous times for photos already and anticipated many more opportunities for photography on the rest of the journey.

In my research for this part of the trip, I had discovered that the mine was situated off something named the Lissadell Road. This turned out to be a vital clue, because there are no signs highlighting the whereabouts of the Argyle mine. While there are numerous other signs posting directions and details to various mines in the area, Rio Tinto clearly don't encourage casual tourists. I had to pay careful attention to side roads but eventually found the one I was looking for. I travelled only a short distance along Lissadell Road before reaching a very large notice board:

ARGYLE DIAMOND MINE

Casual Tours Of The Mine Are Not Conducted

Tour Information Is Available By Contacting

KUNUNURRA VISITOR CENTRE SHIRE OFFICES

I had previously visited the Kununurra Visitor Centre and been told that bus tours from Kununurra were no longer offered. The only official tours of the mine were now incorporated into a plane flight over Lake Argyle, the Purnululu National Park and the Bungle Bungle Range – a flight that included a stopover at the mine – all for a bargain price of $700, plus extras. I was reconciled to the fact that the best I could do would be to drive as close as possible to the mine to take a few photos. I did not expect to meet anyone and somehow gain entry to the site.

Further along Lissadell Road, I turned onto an unmarked road and travelled a short distance to the gates of the mine. This turned out to be a total security lockout for anyone other than a permit-carrying worker. I assumed that the company had installed a photo-scrambling device at the entrance, because I could not take a single clear photograph of the mine's exterior. These shots were in direct contrast to others I had taken earlier in the morning while travelling along the Great Northern Highway. The lack of signage and the difficulty I'd had taking photos registered in me a growing awareness, frustration and curiosity about Rio Tinto's security measures at the mine site.

Back on the Great Northern Highway, I stopped again to take some more photos, now well away from the mine's entrance. My purpose was to find out whether my blurred photos were a camera fault or – as I suspected – the result of external interference by the company, such as a scrambling device. My very clear photos of the rock face of the cliffs adjacent to the highway assuaged my anxiety about camera damage and further spiked my curiosity about security at the mine site.

Back at my car, I noticed the hitchhiker I had seen earlier. Feeling mean for not having stopped previously, I decided to offer this person a lift. I'd first thought the hitchhiker was a man, but then she took her big hat off. She was from New Zealand and said: 'Thanks for stopping. I guess it's karma; I just get dropped here, and you stop to take photos.'

I asked where she was headed 'The Turkey Creek Roadhouse. It's only about an hour from where we are now.'

The next exchange signalled where our talk was headed: 'You're from Victoria. People from down there are different. They are willing to stop and are more friendly and open. They're not as closed as people up here.'

Despite this sweeping generalisation, I decided not to follow through on that issue. Instead, I asked her to tell me more about the differences she was describing. 'Australian men from the north have such shallow views. They have bullshit attitudes and talk that way. They're copies of Crocodile Dundee.'

This exchange set the scene for the next 45 minutes together. Our talk didn't stop, and there were no uncomfortable silences as she told me about places she had visited, people she had met and her views on several political issues.

Significantly, one topic helped me better understand what I had experienced in trying to get information about the Argyle diamond mine. Telling me about her current mission to link up with some Indigenous women at a meeting in Turkey Creek, she also mentioned that the mine site back at Smoke Creek was a women's sacred meeting place. I prompted her to tell me more. She described how, during negotiations between Rio Tinto and leaders of local Indigenous groups about establishing the mine, the women had been sidelined and silenced. I filed away that snippet of information, planning to find sources to check its veracity; it turned out to be true.

In the over 12,000 km I travelled during this mine study, I only picked up one hitchhiker. Despite the brevity of our time together, this comment about the local Indigenous women was a significant catalyst for my thinking. It helped to set a new direction for my subsequent research about the region and the Argyle mine.

Issues

Secret men's business

A newspaper article, 'Diamonds aren't forever: the party's nearly over for Australia's most successful luxury export', confirmed the hitchhiker's account and provided background information about Rio Tinto's early involvement in the lucrative diamond trade.

In August 1979, a group of sample bags arrived in the Derby offices of an exploration group that included CRA (the precursor to Rio Tinto). The bags had come from Smoke Creek, a remote waterway near an Indigenous women's sacred site, 180 km south of Kununurra. By the following year, 1980, an agreement with the local Indigenous people had been signed and a mining lease granted.

The alleged agreement with local Indigenous people happened quite quickly. It is not hard to imagine who held the upper hand in negotiations (clever corporate lawyers) and who were the greatest beneficiaries (owners, managers and shareholders). Probably, local Indigenous people got a raw deal. The song, 'Diamonds are a girl's best friend', did not apply to Indigenous women and girls.

Injurious practices

The headline above claims that diamonds from the Argyle mine are Australia's most successful luxury export. The author, Amanda Hooton, documents how Rio Tinto successfully marketed Argyle's diamonds using a wide variety of techniques. Rio Tinto has turned the best quality pink diamonds into fashionable, desirable and expensive pieces which, in turn, have become symbols of the exclusivity of extreme wealth and purchasing power. Indeed, it has gone even further and rebranded the most common and least desired brown stones:

> [Thirty-five] years ago, nobody wanted a brown diamond.
> People wanted whites, and blues and violets and pinks –
> always pinks – and perhaps, occasionally, a yellow. The
> world's entire supply of brown diamonds, however, were
> classified as 'industrial', and used prosaically in drills, saws
> and machinery.

Argyle set out to change this view via an enormous international marketing drive. Firstly, it changed the name – abandoning the unfortunate 'brown' for the glamorous 'champagne' and 'cognac'.[6]

This is an excellent example of what Marx called 'the noisy sphere of circulation' (i.e., the market). He associated the sphere of circulation with distractions and mystifications that draw attention away from what he called 'the hidden abode of production.'[7] In this abode, the injurious practices of industrial capitalism play out. Certainly, the hidden abode of Rio Tinto's Argyle mine involved injurious practices, not only for workers, but also for local Indigenous people. Both were sacrificed so that the wealthy could adorn themselves with a shiny, very hard, crystalline mineral made of pure carbon.

Sacrificed for diamonds

Meanwhile, back in the towns in the Kimberley closest to the Argyle mine, there is a lived reality far from the gilded enclaves of the super-rich. Halls Creek and Fitzroy Crossing are towns situated on Highway 95, the Great Northern Highway, south of the mine. These two relatively small communities exist today as fabrications of the development and 'civilising' of the region. Halls Creek (population 3,269) has an Indigenous population of

2,425 (74.2 percent of the total). It is profiled on the travel guide website, *Aussie Towns*:

> a strange combination – a relatively modern, predominantly Aboriginal, town servicing the tourism and pastoral industries and a dry, unforgiving ghost town. In 1948 the town was physically moved 16 km to its present location.

The reference to pastoralism casts light on the longer and deeper cultural story of the town and region. A timeline of key events documents a litany of struggles over land use, including examples of conflict between local Indigenous people and pastoralists and multiple massacres involving payback, justified as retribution for previous crimes

Neither Halls Creek nor the smaller Fitzroy Crossing is a wealthy, healthy community, despite the place-marketing that foregrounds exotic tourism hotspots such as the Bungle Bungle Range and the nearby Argyle diamond mine. The 2021 National Census revealed the stark economic reality for people in both towns: the median weekly income for people aged 15 years and over in Halls Creek was $363; in Fitzroy Crossing, it was $600.

My time in this part of the Kimberley was a turning point – a hinge moment. When I visited Morwell, Broken Hill and Roxby Downs, questions about land ownership and the place of Indigenous people had not been raised. In contrast, in the Kimberley, those matters were front and centre. Here in the remote East Kimberley, it was necessary for me to place mining communities within frontier struggles and the unresolved legacies of the occupation and colonisation of the whole country. I also recognised how the land of the Morwell region was secured through a bloody and brutal campaign of land acquisition.

As I left East Kimberley, I juxtaposed the Argyle mine story of Rio Tinto with that of Halls Creek and Fitzroy Crossing. The former story involves great wealth, prestige and power. The latter stories involve histories of violence, abuse and poverty. This is a snapshot of the schism that runs through the nation. For all the symbols and celebrations of creating a nation out of a barren environment dubbed 'terra nullius', there is the counter-narrative of the heavy toll taken on the lives and the lived culture of Indigenous people – still experienced today.

The Argyle mine has now closed and is apparently undergoing rehabilitation in line with the company's sustainability proclamations. I doubt that I will travel back to see whether it is properly honouring its promises of 'respectfully closing and rehabilitating the mine and returning the land to its traditional custodians'. However, the signs are bleak.

8.

Technological behemoth: Mount Whaleback (WA)

Land of the Palyku language group

Overview

Newman is a mining town in the East Pilbara of WA. Newman Operations is the title of two BHP mining sites: Newman West and Newman East. These sites are integrated into BHP's Pilbara network by a rail system that terminates at the coastal town of Port Hedland. The 2021 census gives the overall population as 4,239 and the Indigenous population as 556.

The town and the mines are close to the Little Sandy Desert, home to some of the last nomadic people of the Manyjilyjarra language group. This is an arid region with very little annual rainfall and very high summer temperatures.

Vast deposits of iron ore were discovered at Mount Whaleback in the 1950s, but the discovery was kept secret because of an international embargo on the export of iron ore, lifted in 1960. Mining began at Newman in 1967. A purpose-built company town, Newman is six km west of the mine and is designed to cater for the varied needs of industry, the workforce and their families. The design is classically pragmatic. A small, centrally located shopping centre comprises stores that accommodate the most practical and immediate needs of the population.

A privately owned, heavy freight railway line caters for long trains, powerful diesel engines and the transport of enormous loads of ore. Given the combined challenges – the distance from a shipping centre, the rugged terrain to be crossed and the extremes in weather conditions, which include both monsoon-driven floods and very high ground temperatures – a well-maintained rail system is an important feature of the mining industry at this location.

The line is 426 km long, traversing long sections of relatively steep terrain:

> A typical train will have six, 6,000 horsepower locomotives pulling more than 26,000 tonnes of ore. Most trains are 208 cars, each carrying approximately 125 tonnes of ore. The trains are up to 3.75 kilometres long and the journey from Newman to Port Hedland takes approximately eight hours.[1]

On 21 June 2001, this route registered a world record for the heaviest and longest train: a train and 682 wagons, altogether weighing 99,734 tons, ran for 275 km between Yandi and Port Hedland. The train was 7.3 km long and carried 82,000 tons of iron ore. It's certainly impressive.

My visit

On 8 August 2015, I travelled from Port Hedland on the coast towards Newman and Mount Whaleback at the edge of the desert. I had two route choices: the faster and more conventional route, via the sealed tarmac of Highway 95, or a gravel road, known as Route 138, via the towns of Marble Bar and Nullagine. I chose the latter because it allowed me to take a side trip to an abandoned airfield at Corunna Downs, approximately 34 km south of Marble Bar.

Corunna Downs is a red dirt landscape strewn with iron ore rocks, spinifex, wire grass, saltbush and Mallee shrubland. It held a top-secret airfield during WWII, including a base where my father was stationed for a short time as an RAAF radio operator. The former airfield's two gravel runways are in surprisingly good condition, given the harsh environment and the 70 years since they were operational. In this extremely remote location, I was able to imagine what it was like during my father's short time here so long ago, with Japanese planes frantically trying to find the location. The fact that the Japanese planes were not successful in locating the airbase highlights the extreme remoteness of this place.

After a time back on Route 138, I stopped in the tiny town of Nullagine, a former gold mining site now dubbed the Prospectors Patch. It is also the location of the Irrungadji Aboriginal community and local representatives of the Martu people, traditional occupants of the region.

The town recently experienced a revival in gold mining activity. During my short stopover, I quickly came to realise that there was direct and overt separation between the Indigenous population and other members of the population. While I was eating a meal at the hotel, an Indigenous man who tried to gain entry was quickly walked off the premises. The rationale, according to the person serving at the bar, was that the hotel was simply operating under government policy about who should not be served alcohol. His response to my questions struck me as an example of hiding behind a legalistic smokescreen. The way the eviction was executed appeared excessively forceful and brutal. There was no discussion. The moment the man appeared at the door and took only a few steps inside, he was grabbed, spun around and evicted. I was unused to such overt and unapologetic expressions of racism and was left with the feeling of being 'in another country.'

My subsequent quick trip around the tiny town reinforced my growing awareness of the practice of racial separation. At the Lynas Lookout, gaining a better view of Nullagine and the adjacent landscape, I heard music booming up from a small cluster of houses near the base of the lookout. My curiosity spiked, I drove over a culvert and into what was evidently a separate micro-community. As I crossed the culvert, a dog rushed up to my vehicle, barking loudly and aggressively. Within moments, the dog was joined by a second, then a third, fourth, fifth and sixth, combining into a ferocious tangle of snapping and snarling canine aggression. There was no way I was going to stop and step out of my vehicle. I understood this experience as a sign that I was not welcome and that I should move on. This thought was reinforced by the fact that a group of four or five people were standing together and talking while all this commotion occurred. They appeared to neither notice nor care about my presence and the disturbance it had created.

I booked into an accommodation complex on the outskirts of Newman catering for tourists and for workers at the mine who are not part of BHP Billiton's FIFO workforce. My choice of hotel was both fortunate and strategic. During my two-night stay, I was able to talk to people who had useful insights about work in the mine and life in the town. Other schisms emerged.

I had a particularly revealing discussion with a couple who were living permanently at the complex and were also, originally, from Victoria. During a previous trip, while on a break from farming, they had stopped at the complex. The man had been offered a position as a maintenance worker, which he accepted. When they returned to Newman, the woman successfully applied for a kitchen hand position with BHP Billiton within the mine site complex. When she arrived at the site to begin work, she was stopped at the entrance while two security staff had an extended discussion with a mine official. The woman was then told that she should not have been offered the position, because the company policy was not to employ Newman residents. The only way she could work there was on the basis on which she had been offered the position: as a FIFO worker. This she eventually decided to do. When we talked, she was on her one-week break between two weekly 12-hours-per-day rosters inside the FIFO accommodation.

This discussion revealed the strict policy regime governing FIFO work and the practice of separation between mine workers and the town's general population – a practice that is widespread in Australia. I wondered why the company policy reinforced separation between the mine workers and company functions and the day-to-day life of people in Newman.

I had two very different types of interaction featuring Indigenous people. In Nullagine, I had witnessed the eviction of an Indigenous man from the local hotel. That event appeared riddled with contradictions and deep-seated prejudice. The next morning, I drove through the tiny Indigenous area of

Nullagine. It felt like a place where there was a genuine racial divide, socially and geographically. I was relieved to drive away. Later, I wondered whether it was it just the dogs, and my sense of being an unwelcome intruder, that led me to feel so relieved. Was there more to it? I returned to my project hinge point with the hitch hiker. Perhaps my will to escape is a typical white settler response to Indigenous people who are living with the deprivations associated with ongoing colonisation. Turn away. Go away. Unpacking my discomfort made me intensely aware of the gulf between me and Indigenous people. It made me even more determined to seek out and try to understand their relationship to mining.

In contrast, in Newman later that same day, I easily and comfortably engaged in an extended discussion with a couple who told me how welcome they felt on coming to live in Newman. They spoke about some of the trials and tribulations of life for FIFO workers in mining. Within these occupational, gendered and racial divisions, I felt very aware of fitting comfortably within an urban white, middle-class, professional demographic. And I felt a long, long way from the world of remote workers and particularly of Indigenous people who embody a cultural heritage reaching back millennia.

Not long before sunset, I drove into Newman to look around the town and its shopping centre and to seek out a general vantage point overlooking the area. This was a place known as the Radio Hill Lookout, located strategically at a mid-point between the two key features, with the town on one side and mine site on the other.

On my initial visit, I also discovered the Newman Visitor Centre, where there was a display board about booking a place on a tour of the mine site. At 8.45 the next morning, I went back to the Visitor Centre to take part in the daily tour. Following company directives, I wore my hiking boots, long-sleeved top and sturdy trousers.

Our tour began with the obligatory welcomes, explanations of the itinerary and reminders about safety considerations while outside the vehicle and in the open within the mine site. As we drove to our first vantage point, our tour guide provided a

Rocks consisting of 68% iron ore at Mt Whaleback, W.A.

general overview and potted history of the mine. This spiel made it clear that we were getting a company-focused pitch structured for visitors with little or no experience of the workings of major industrial mine sites. I would call this Mining BHP 101.

At the lookout, our guide gave a general description of the key features that we could observe: the massive pit, five km long, 1.5 km wide and 0.5 km deep; loading depots for trains; and numerous buildings housing equipment and key workers. One innocuous, dust-covered, metal building was highlighted as perhaps the most important place in the whole pit. This was where industrial chemists, geologists and accountants teamed up. Their task was to assess the quality of deposits about to be loaded onto trains. This work involved checking iron content and purity levels that would then be matched with specific orders or bids from overseas buyers. The guide informed us that the iron content in the ore was around 68 percent, generally extremely high quality, and thus had a very high market value. This snippet of information, fusing geology, physics and economics, grabbed my attention. When our guide had finished the overview, I walked over to a cluster of rocks adjacent to the car park and tested for myself the relative weight of one rock, to get a better understanding of what we had been told. I have never picked up a rock that was so heavy relative to its size.

Another important snippet of information from this tour related to the role technicians and engineers play in automating work in and beyond the pit. We learned of efforts to develop automated systems that would provide driverless trucks and trains and automated drones carrying high-level visual devices for checking machinery and rail lines. Further information, received and monitored via an increasing number of recording devices, was being channelled through a high-tech resource in Perth, known as the Integrated Remote Operations Centre (IROC). The Centre was launched in 2013, two years before my trip. At the time of its introduction, the company provided the following description of the scope of work at IROC:

> Our Integrated Remote Operations Centre...is also centrally located. IROC enables staff to coordinate, from Perth, the near-term scheduling, planning, and controlling of our mine, rail and port operations.[2]

Here we see another example of remote control, pointing to the changing nature of the mining workforce.

I spent the rest of the day exploring the outside perimeter of the mine, the shopping centre and what I understood to be the bulk of residential areas in the town. My initial impression, based on this cursory overview and casual chats with some people working in the business centre, was that Newman was a small, well-serviced, neat and tidy town.

Only as I was leaving Newman next morning, heading for Tom Price, another Pilbara mine site, did I become aware of a small cluster of about a dozen houses on the very outskirts of the north-western side of the town. This was the Parnpajinya community, physically separated from the rest of the town. I didn't stop to meet anyone or turn around to drive into the settlement. I felt that this would have been an unjustifiable intrusion. I simply filed this information about Parnpajinya community away, knowing that I would need to access other sources to learn more about the people living there. Subsequently, with ample time to reflect on my hesitancy, I became aware of some residual dissonance left over from my time in Nullagine.

Newman – a town divided

The local tug of war

Shire officials, with their mandate and responsibility to cater for rate-paying citizens, have a vested interest in positive accounts of their region and municipalities. Newman is projected as a progressive showcase:

> Newman has entered a new era. Just ask the long-term residents of Newman who have seen extraordinary changes to the town in the heart of the Pilbara they call home. Today, Newman is a revitalised, modern municipality and one of the key regional centres of Western Australia's enormous Pilbara region. The July completion of Newman's Town Square – with its nine-metre outdoor screen – was the cherry on top of the ambitious Newman Town Centre Revitalisation Plan; the blueprint which visualised the transformation of Newman into the modern, rejuvenated, and revamped town that exists today.[3]

The target audience for the statement probably includes potential investors in commercial properties, individuals and families considering moving into the town, families and businesses already located there and, last but not least, tourists.

There are tensions, divisions and silences within the shire's pitch. Perhaps the most potent and suggestive issue is the growing number of empty and unkempt houses within the town:

- More than 150 houses in a visible state of disrepair and/ or empty.
- Empty houses as targets of vandals and sites for antisocial behaviour.

- A disjuncture between BHP and the WA Government's Department of Housing about responsibilities for appropriate management.
- Growing concerns about the lack of a viable future in the region for the rising generation of teenagers.

The 'emptying-out' of the town is evident in demographics data from the 2006, 2011, 2016 and 2020–21 National Census. After peaking in 2011 at 5,478, the population declined to 4,239 in 20/21.[4] The trend aligns with shifts in the number of Newman residents employed locally.

The changes unfolding in Newman merge within a complex historical and spatial dynamic. Many conflicting vested interests compete at multiple levels.

In the first instance, this involves a tug of war between residents and regional officials, on one side, and corporate mining on the other. Between these opposing groups are state and federal levels of government.

Residents and Shire of Pilbara officials are jointly motivated by concerns about Newman's public profile, a status factor that has multiple forms of economically vested interests. For residents, this includes property values, individual and community safety and welfare concerns and uncertainties about the town's long-term viability.

Contrasted to this is configuration of industrial and government preoccupations about the management of the mine's workforce. This involves concerns about facilitating stability and certainty within the mine worksite. Concretely and specifically, this tension becomes visible in the management and control measures of the FIFO workforce.

FIFO workers

In 2004, BHP won approval to build a camp for its growing contingent of FIFO workers. The company went on record declaring that this housing arrangement was to be a short-term measure, with demobilisation to begin in 2007. This implied that the company's longer-term management strategy for its workforce was to eventually house workers within the town.

That did not occur.

Ten years on, in 2015, the company announced plans to apply to extend its lease for a further 20 years. The timing of this development was problematic, occurring when an increasing number of company owned houses in the town had become vacant. A locally based backlash followed, neatly summarised in the blunt assessment of a long-term resident, Paul Foster: 'FIFO has never done any good for the town.' The Shire of East Pilbara's CEO, Allen Cooper, supported this view in principle, asserting that the company had a 'social obligation' to wind back the camp and to house more workers in the town:

> The company has 300, maybe 400, empty accommodation units in town that could be used for residential employees, that will support the town rather than a FIFO camp where no-one mixes.

BHP continued to invest in maintaining the housing of FIFO workers in the Kurra Camp for a further five years. At the start of 2020, the company finally began the process of dismantling its camp infrastructure.[5]

The tensions embedded within this example illustrate the power dynamics involved. Panning out a little, these tensions and the vested interests of different parties were on display in another event that occurred within this time frame.

In February 2013, the Australian Government's House of Representatives Standing Committee on Regional Australia presented findings of an inquiry, *Cancer of the Bush or Salvation for our Cities?*[6] This document reported on an investigation into the impacts of the mining industries 'fly-in, fly-out/drive-in drive-out' (FIFO/DIDO) work practices. The title of the report, posed as a question, was designed to dramatise two themes: concerns about FIFO/DIDO work practices on specific mining communities, in contrast to supporting and underwriting big industry by moving workers from major population centres to remote or regional locations.

During the release of findings, a summative media release included the suggestion that, if the various recommendations were accepted, this 'can build stronger inland regional communities alongside a strong resources industry'.[7]

In October 2021, the Australian Mining Cities Alliance (AMCA) released a statement about the *Cancer of the Bush or Salvation for our Cities?* report. It expressed dissatisfaction and annoyance at the lack of follow-through on the different recommendations:

> Ten years later as the Chair of the Australian Mining Cities Alliance (AMCA) and Mayor of the City of Kalgoorlie–Boulder, John Bowler reflected last week on the lack of progress by the Commonwealth and State Governments to make change. 'This issue has been mulled over by various governments for years and while there are plenty of reports and recommendations to show for it, not enough real progress has been made,' he said.[8]

This statement highlights the relative roles of the main parties. Local councils and communities and big business/mining companies are clearly cast in opposition. Significantly, commonwealth and state governments occupy an ambiguous position somewhere between the two. While representing citizens in general, the two top tiers of government are also major beneficiaries of royalties from mining companies. That ambiguity appears to be a significant factor in the problems identified within the AMCA statement.

FIFO mine workers are subject to wide-ranging pressures and complexities resulting from long distance travel and ongoing relocation. Many accounts detail the scope of these forces and the impacts they have on FIFO workers' lives. Leigo and Marsellos have drawn from results of research to outline some the difficulties, challenges and safety issues encountered and documented by a seasoned mine worker, Luke Baker. Known on social media as 'FIFO Man', Baker has stressed the mental pressures associated with FIFO practices and asserted that workers experience a potent mix of pressures, 'due to the style of work, the isolation, the remoteness and the amount of time that we're away from home'.

Matthew, a 16-year veteran of the FIFO arrangement, rein-forces these views. In the *Cancer of the Bush* Inquiry, he was asked about living in a remote town site next to a mine:

> The thought of living in some small town in the
> middle of nowhere is not a realistic option where
> services and amenities are next to non-existent. I
> wouldn't live in a remote area to work on a mine site. I
> work FIFO for the above benefits, not the drawback of
> living in a small community.[9]

At the extreme end of such perspectives about the FIFO life-style are the cases of severe health breakdowns and the incidence of worker suicide within the mining industry. A recent research report examining the mental health and wellbeing of FIFO workers showed that one-third of FIFO workers experience high or very high levels of psychological distress, compared to only 17 per cent of non-FIFO workers.

The research report covered 3,000 FIFO workers and found that FIFO workers may be more prone to suicide.

Meredith, Rush and Robinson conducted a meta-analysis of the research about the impact of FIFO/DIDO practices on work-ers' families. Five major themes emerged from their survey: family functioning; wellbeing, including the mental health of the FIFO worker and their home parent/partner; couple re-lationships; parenting; and the effects on children. Meredith, Rush and Robinson point out:

> The ability of family members to enjoy the benefits and
> manage the challenges…can significantly influence
> the effect of FIFO on children and family relationships.
> Resilience in the transition to FIFO employment
> depends on a number of factors, including: the ability
> of family members to adapt to the changed conditions
> of a FIFO lifestyle; the at-home partner's local support
> network; and the support and flexibility offered by the
> FIFO worker's employer.[10]

This work helps to clarify the complexity of the interlacing factors that are at play in the FIFO lifestyles maintained by mine workers and their families. But it does not attend to the problems experienced – mainly by women FIFO workers.

In 2021, women made up 19.2 percent of the FIFO/DIDO workforce. A recent WA Parliamentary Inquiry examined sexual harassment in the FIFO industry. This led to the report called *Enough is Enough*. It showed that sexual harassment is rife and pointed to many cultural problems, including abuse of power, misuse of alcohol, gender imbalance and the normalisation of sexual harassment. It also showed that complaints are either ignored or treated ineffectively, that reporting systems are inadequate, and that people in leadership roles have a poor understanding of the issue.

Since that report, there have been many calls for more leadership and better communication from the mining sector, as well as for cultural change and better recruitment, working arrangements and facilities for women in the workplace. In February 2022, the WA Government Department of Mines, Industry Regulation and Safety issued three new Codes of Practice:

- The Code of Practice on Workplace Behaviour – covering misconduct, prolonged conflict, discrimination, harassment, sexual harassment and bullying
- The Code of Practice on Psychosocial Hazards in the Workplace – including violence, aggression, fatigue, burnout, stress and trauma
- The Code of Practice on Violence and Aggression at Work – provides guidance where workers may be exposed to physical assault, verbal abuse, threats, intimidation and harassment.[11]

Also, in April 2019, the Department of Mines, Industry Regulation and Safety had issued another Code of Conduct called 'Mentally healthy workplaces for FIFO workers in the resources and construction sectors'.[12]

We are yet to see whether the FIFO/DIDO industry responds in a substantive manner or just tinkers at the edges and uses puff pieces to ward off further criticism.

On the other side of the ledger, BHP's position can be interpreted through traditional industrial perspectives. The company's concern is about its bottom line: profit. The generation of profit results, in part, from the company's capacity to extract surplus value from its workers. FIFO work is a mechanism of control and coercion whereby the lives of workers are both heavily regulated and integrated into the company's production processes.

There are many ways in which these outcomes are produced. Long 12-hour shifts limit time for recreation and recuperation. Strict codes of supervision increase the capacity of company supervisors to monitor workers' behaviour outside work hours. Such measures have recently been taken to an extreme with an announcement that managers in BHP's mining camps have been given authority to search miners' rooms. This development runs in tandem with a company announcement about limitations on alcohol use within camps.

In his studies of mining in the Pilbara, labour historian Alexis Vassiley documented five decades of changes to unionism and industrial procedures in mining in the Pilbara. From the 1970s to the mid-1980s, union militancy generated significant gains for workers. Subsequently, more moderate strategies adopted by union officials led to a loss of relative power in industrial relations. The emergence of FIFO, as a management technique, has accentuated this trend. Vassiley concludes:

> FIFO has made unionisation more difficult as it isolates workers. Twelve-hour shifts on an on-swing, with close surveillance by management is not conducive to union organising... In short: unions out, FIFO in.[13]

Rainnie and colleagues call this move to use a large FIFO workforce the 'third spatial fix'. The 'first spatial fix' involved closed towns, in which the company provided the resources and the management. The 'second spatial fix' was a period when workers were encouraged to purchase their homes under schemes controlled by state governments. The third fix, involving FIFO camps, has been the source of tension between those locals who became ensconced in the second fix and the company, BHP. The next section outlines what can be classed as a fourth spatial fix: a production process that is increasingly extended across space.

The fourth spatial fix

In late 2019, the *Sydney Morning Herald* published an article by Nick Toscano titled, 'Rise of the machines: Miners race towards automation'. It began:

> There's a photo making its way around the top ranks of BHP at the moment. It's an aerial picture from Jimblebar, one of the company's biggest mines in the Pilbara. It shows a truck following a set of tyre marks, as straight as a train track, etched into the earth from the thousands of trips before it.
>
> The reason staff at BHP are emailing the unremarkable photo to each other is that the truck is autonomous – meaning it's driverless – and the tyre marks tell much about why these vehicles are being rolled out across the miner's haulage fleet.[14]

This anecdote takes us into a range of developments that have profound effects on the way that industries are changing and, therefore, on how such changes need to be understood and critically analysed. The key issue involves the introduction of 'autonomous' machinery. This is happening at many different levels of industry and has implications for the way business is being conducted and is likely to change. Leading mining companies Rio Tinto and BHP are now locked into high-tech competition to produce the next generation of industrial hardware and associated information systems and programs.

Justified to shareholders as a necessary development in anticipation of the inevitable downturn in demand for iron ore, companies expanded their use of data collection, collation and analysis as a key production strategy.

In December 2019, Jamie Bennett, Director of BHP Innovation Centre, presented a paper titled 'Innovating for a data-driven future'. He used the concept of real-time scheduling, a data-based method that is being used by 'mine schedulers' to 'analyse and combine disparate data sets to improve load and haul operations'. The data is assisting company analysts and planners to create a single-system mode of production, underpinned by three themes: predictability, reliability and stability.

These developments and aspirations help to explain the emergence of a fourth spatial fix that is difficult to recognise because it comprises three separate production sites located well apart from each other: the Perth group innovation centre, which is focused on software development; the Welshpool (a Perth suburb) site, where hardware and software are initially tested; and Newman's Eastern Ridge Centre, where developments are field tested 'operationally'.

This is an excellent example of the complexity of contemporary, high-tech mining. Tucked away in a laboratory in the very heart of Perth's CBD is the technological, information-based nerve centre. Like so many other forms of contemporary high-tech industry, this place focuses on machines and techniques designed to streamline production processes. After simulation testing, actual field testing occurs over 1,000 kms away at the Eastern Ridge Centre. This science driven process involves the integrated stages of conceptualisation, design, prototype building and testing and then field testing designed to provide data-driven feedback.

Issues

Local fragmentation and command from a distance

Newman is also the administration centre for the Shire of East Pilbara, which is – by area – Australia's largest shire. Politically, the town is positioned at the centre of two related but very different types of institution: mining companies on the one hand and local government management on the other. The companies, operating as businesses within the local and international marketplace of mining, focus on the bottom line of their financial ledger: profit or loss. The local government authority has a mandate and a responsibility for the welfare of citizens/ residents and visitors – including facilities, essential services, maintenance and governance of public spaces and facilities. In Newman, the tensions are building between these two different institutional imperatives.

In her monologue at the lookout, the tour guide had noted that BHP Billiton is engaged in a major restructuring and streamlining process. The company is developing and introducing many automated processes and facilities. As this process advances, many services and roles that have previously been localised, or performed in situ, are now being centralised in the IROC in Perth. In mid-2019, journalist Vanessa Zhou wrote:

> BHP will potentially introduce up to 500 autonomous trucks at its Australian open-cut operations, a tenfold increase on the company's existing fleet at the Jimblebar mine in the Pilbara.[15]

Centrally controlled automated systems result in labour-saving outcomes for the company but also reduce the numbers of workers and community members in specific locations. The pressure building inside this set of tensions has been unleashed within the town of Newman.

There are multiple signs of these developments, including the many empty and rundown houses in the town. Since the 2016 census, shire officials and several leading politicians have been lobbying BHP to integrate FIFO workers into Newman's mainstream population. This is a protracted struggle.

The Shire of East Pilbara's website says:

> The mining sector dominates the Shire of East Pilbara economic landscape. Mining is estimated to contribute $16,017 billion (89%) of total output generated within the Shire.

Plenty of money is clearly flowing through the area, but it is not at all clear how much flows to the shire itself, let alone to local community projects. Further, the shire's efforts to build local culture are facing an uphill battle, given BHP Billiton's use of FIFO workers and centrally controlled automated systems. The separation between the town and the mine is growing dramatically. And we are yet to see the outcomes of the project to more closely integrate FIFO workers with the local community.

This issue playing out in Newman is also likely to be played out in numerous other FIFO mining sites. Given the growing understanding about the problems created by FIFO work practices, Newman may well become a test case for other mining communities.

Expelled from their place

The second major issue from this Newman story is the wellbeing and security of the local Indigenous population. Although I didn't have the opportunity to meet any people from the Parnpajinya community, others have done so and published their impressions. I was able to learn from these. Marta Pascual Juanola's article, 'Welcome to the slums on the very edge of WA's mining epicentre',[16] is an account of the lives and views of several people living in Parnpajinya and a disturbing presentation of the tensions that exist between government authorities, mega-sized multinational industries and representatives of the Indigenous people who have occupied the region for tens of thousands of years.

The Parnpajinya community was established by the Martu people, who were originally from the Western Desert. Initially, Parnpajinya was a settlement adjacent to the Mount Whaleback miners' camp. In 1981, the Shire of East Pilbara purchased the miners' camp from the mining company, and Newman was formally established as a town. However, Parnpajinya was not part of this arrangement, meaning that provision of basic town services did not apply there.

Several pressing questions and issues arise. Was this arrangement worked out in conjunction and consultation with the people of Parnpajinya? If so, what legal arrangements were put in place? Conversely, was this an arrangement worked out exclusively by the state government and the mining company?

If so, were any subsequent arrangements made with the leaders of Parnpajinya that have been carried over into current times?

In 2019, the state government began a process of moving people from Parnpajinya into vacant houses within Newman, demolishing and removing the newly vacated Parnpajinya houses. Subsequent struggles and resistance to moving by those remaining have been about using funding from the Pilbara Cities Investment Project for fixing up and servicing Parnpajinya. The contentious issue, in this case, is whether funds should be used to refurbish and maintain Parnpajinya's houses or whether to continue with arrangements to move people into vacant houses in Newman.

Understanding the complexity of this issue requires a capacity to embrace the fact that there are very different perspectives and micro-politics in play. The state government has a policy of closing settlements such as Parnpajinya, and it has a continuing program of social and cultural 'integration'. This overlooks the fact that Parnpajinya is an important stopover place for many Martu people who sometimes live at Jigalong, Pumnu and Parrngurr communities beyond Newman. Further, Newman is the headquarters for the Martu people's management group, known as the Kanyirninpa Jukurrpa or KJ. This group is vested with the responsibility to coordinate the movement of Martu people back to traditional land, a movement known as the 'coming back'. In a formal and legal arrangement, this process involves people of the Martu returning to undertake land management programs over the vast arid region and to help prevent large-scale, destructive wildfires through a process of small locations burning. This is a long established and effective method of land management and is vital in the process of protecting endangered species, including the greater bilby and northern quoll.

I have treated these issues as separate. Substantively, however, they are fused within a larger cultural and political framework. BHP Billiton, local and state governments and the Martu people of Parnpajinya exist within a state of asymmetrical tension that, in the short term, dates back to the time a lease was granted for mining to begin. In the longer term, these tensions date back to colonisation itself.

9.

'Grinding poverty alongside relative affluence'. Kalgoorlie–Boulder (WA)

Land of Wangkathaa language group

Overview

On 15 February 2010, the NASA Earth Observatory generated an image of Kalgoorlie, the adjacent Fimiston open pit mine – locally known as the Super Pit – and a vast area of brown, arid land stretching in all directions beyond these two central features. NASA's satellite-based image offers a unique overview of this mining location. Kalgoorlie is located approximately 600 km east of Perth, in what is known as the Eastern Goldfields region of WA. A gold mining region, the area covered by this image is home to nine active mines. It is one of the premier gold mining sites in WA and has maintained that status for over a century. The 2021 census shows an overall population of 29,306 and an Indigenous population of 2,244.

Located in the Kalgoorlie–Boulder region of the Eastern Goldfields, the Golden Mile was a term used to describe an approximate square mile of land containing a number of mines: Golden Horseshoe, Great Boulder, Ivanhoe, Hannan's Star, Boulder Main Reef and Chaffers. A recent estimate of gold extracted from this area totals 60 million ounces, with a relative value in current terms of $100 billion.

Gold was discovered in Coolgardie in 1892. A gold rush quickly followed, and a township developed and grew. Within six years, there was an estimated population of approximately 5,000 people and a municipality with many mines, hotels and businesses. Meanwhile, 40 km to the north-east, the embryonic townships of Kalgoorlie and Boulder were growing, following the discovery of gold deposits in June 1893.

The 1890s was a watershed in WA's economic history because of the discovery of gold on the Eastern Goldfields. In just one decade, the small, rural-based economy saw a four-fold increase in population and a massive increase in infrastructure as capital became available. From just 48,000 people in 1890, the population climbed to 180,000 in 1901.

This rapid population growth was the catalyst for both serious problems and, eventually, the development of essential services for those in the goldfields and in the pastoral areas between there and Perth.

A combination of overcrowded living and camping conditions, with deficient sanitation facilities and a lack of clean water, primed the region for disease and chronic illness. In February 1895, the Kalgoorlie Progress Committee sent a telegram to the WA Premier, John Forrest: 'Health of town most unsatisfactory. Fever spreading, deaths daily and business threatened. No sanitary measures enforced or enforceable'. This was a report about a typhoid epidemic that was spreading through the goldfields. Forrest engaged Charles Yelverton O'Connor, an engineer with a diverse portfolio of infrastructure achievements, to develop a strategy for getting a reliable and adequate water supply into the Eastern Goldfields. O'Connor's response was a plan to divert water from the Helena River, 500 km away in the Darling Ranges, to the goldfield towns.

In what became the Coolgardie Water Supply Scheme, water from near the coast – where, currently, the annual average rainfall is 800 mm per annum – was to be piped to the arid goldfields, where the average rainfall is approximately 200 mm per annum. Forrest backed the scheme enthusiastically and approved and funded it via the *Coolgardie Goldfields Water Supply Loan Act 1896*. Construction began in 1896 of a dam, now known as Lake CY

O'Connor, in the Darling Ranges and a 530 km pipeline, consisting of interlocking steel pipes and eight pumping stations, to drive water through the system. Both were completed in 1903. The system is still in operation and is now used to supply water to several towns along its route. In a tragic twist in this narrative of an essential and lasting legacy, O'Connor, subjected to a cocktail of pressures, criticisms and hard work, took his own life on 10 March 1902.

For the next 80 years, underground mining continued within and beyond Kalgoorlie's Golden Mile. During this time, disruptions occurred; miners left during the two World Wars and there were riots involving migrant miners and 'locals' in 1934. This dispute signifies the existence of deep-seated tensions between different groups that may, on occasions, escalate into violent conflict.[1]

In 1950, a series of amalgamations between companies marked the start of a movement towards industrially diverse and robust mega-organisations.

 Later, during the 1960s and 1970s, research and development and the application of processes in which scientific developments fused with engineering and marketing increased technological sophistication within the mining sector. A prime example was the importation of techniques from South Africa that made possible new processes of extraction from previously worked deposits.

As a result of such developments in mining's productive techniques and industrial organisation, Alan Bond, a Perth-based entrepreneur, put in place a grand plan to consolidate the Golden Mile's independent leases to begin open pit mining. Following a complicated set of industrial negotiations, rationalisations and amalgamations that culminated in March 1989, Kalgoorlie Consolidated Gold Mines (KCGM) was registered. What followed was the start of a large open pit, now known as the Super Pit, and the upgrading of the processing and roasting technique and plant. In 2014, the 25th anniversary of KCGM, the company announced that the 16 millionth ounce of gold had been poured; since mining began in the Golden Mile in 1893, 58,000,000 ounces of gold had been extracted.

In specific terms, Kalgoorlie's Super Pit is Australia's second largest mine, behind the Boddington Gold Mine, also located in WA. The Kalgoorlie pit is 3.5 km in length, 1.5 km across and over 600 m deep. The mine set a production benchmark of 800,000 ounces of gold until 2017–2018, when a series of major wall collapses slowed production, causing the loss of over 150 permanent positions.

In December 2019, two Australian-based companies, Northern Star Resources and Saracen Mineral Holdings, purchased the joint 50 percent ownership arrangement from Newmont Goldcorp and Barrick Gold. Subsequently, the two companies merged and formed Northern Star Resources Limited.

My visit

On 17 August 2015, I took a guided tour into the Super Pit. I stood in the middle of Hannan Street, the showpiece of this historic city, among the grand federation buildings, with a group of about 20 people booked to go on the tour. We were all dressed appropriately: long-sleeved tops and strong, sturdy footwear (no sign of thongs anywhere in this group). We were ushered aboard our bus, met our tour guide and were introduced to our bus driver, who – greeting us with a wave but without turning to look at us – issued an explanation of what we would be doing during the next couple of hours, where we would be taken and how we must behave. It felt a little like being on a school excursion.

The satellite image referenced at the beginning of this chapter confirms that, in cosmic terms, there is only a wafer-thin space between city and mine. The significance of that fact would later become much more vivid and audible when we witnessed blasting deep within the pit.

As the bus wound its way to the upper rim of the mine, our tour guide provided us with a cryptic account of the history of mining within the Golden Mile, beginning with the relatively primitive, labour-intensive and dangerous tunnelling, blasting and removal of earth and the sifting and sorting of extracted material. We were like any typical class or group of learners: some were listening, others were looking out the windows, a few were chatting among themselves, and one or two, inevitably, were staring at their mobile phones.

Our first stop was at a dumping site for bits and pieces of the detritus from the mine shafts from what is called the Golden Mile Mark – the early years. At the dumping site, rock, wood, metal piping, twisted pieces of iron and what appeared to be a broken ceramic pipe lay strewn across the entire area. It was unsettling to think that this material had been located hundreds of metres beneath the surface. More unsettling still was the thought of the laborious effort it must have taken to collect, fashion and transport these necessary basic support structures of the tunnels and shafts of the separate mines.

Our second stop was within a large and level workstation where several ore-carrying vehicles were assembled. Workers were washing some of these machines and servicing and maintaining others. Many tyres for these massive vehicles are assembled here. These tyres cost over $30,000 each. Everything about this collection of machinery and spare parts is huge and expensive. Unlike the picks, shovels, sticks of dynamite and modest-sized rail carts of Mining Mark 1, these Caterpillar haul trucks cost many millions to purchase, fuel and maintain. They can carry loads up to 230 tonnes in weight.

At our next stop, we were told that we were about to watch a blast deep inside the pit. Our guide then provided a very distilled account of the blasting procedure. This was useful to the extent that it left us – at least those of us who were interested and still listening – in no doubt that there was nothing random or haphazard about what we were soon to witness. Blasting is a carefully coordinated process. It involves production geologists, who seek out lode-bearing seams. Preliminary checks are then performed by void managers – managers of areas subject to previous underground mining. Planning engineers perform pre-blast site preparation, then a blast team does site preparation. A coordinator, who has assessed the suitability of the weather and the wind direction and has ensured that the site is cleared of all personnel, does a blast-management check and approval.

While waiting for the blasting to begin, I edged out as far as possible from our viewing platform to peer down into the pit.

Beneath us was a distinctly green pool of water. Curious about this, I took the chance to ask the tour guide. He explained that water in the pit is heavily mineralised through processes of natural leaching. Water leakage, such as had formed the pool beneath us, was drained and used for settling dust on the roads within the pit, thus making the surface more stable for the ore-carrying trucks. Pit-leached water was used to wash down the ore trucks. Having stored those snippets of information away, I subsequently discovered that ore trucks rarely last beyond five years, because of severe rusting. I wondered whether such production wear-and-tear became a company tax write-off.

This blasting was, appropriately, the final part of our tour. After the dust settled, when movement within the pit had recommenced, we returned to the bus.

After returning to Hannan Street and handing back my protective glasses, hard hat and vest, I made my way to the Museum of the Goldfields. Housed on the museum site is the Eastern Goldfields Miners Memorial, which is dedicated to those who lost their lives while mining. Currently, 1,484 names are listed. While I was writing this account of the Eastern Goldfields, another miner died because of an accident at the Karari-Dervish underground mine, 120 km north-east of Kalgoorlie–Boulder. In due course, his name will be added to the Eastern Goldfields Miners' Memorial, extending further the register of mining's costly legacy.

Issues

Misleading boasting and boosting

There is great deal of hype about Kalgoorlie's status as a nationally and internationally significant mining location. This is underscored by a tight synthesis between mining companies and local and state governments. Their concern has always been to represent mining operations to the public in the most positive ways. In the idiom of popular culture, 'bigger than Texas' is a phrase about an attitude of brashness, bravado, bold claims and out of the ordinary size. In Australia, a 'bigger than Texas' sensibility is regularly used to describe Kalgoorlie in mainstream publications and on social media websites; the advertising associated with a tourist activity called the Golden Quest Discovery Trail describes Kalgoorlie as:

> Australia's largest outback city, and one of the most famous gold mining centres on the planet. Its history is intimately linked with the fortunes of Western Australia and, indeed, of Australia as a nation.[2]

An example of the way this hype has evolved, and is ongoing, is found in the narrative of KCGM and Fimiston Open Pit, the Super Pit.

This narrative began in March 1989, when KCGM was formally registered. The joint venture was an agreement between Homestake Gold of Australia and Normandy Mining. In the first year of operations, the Gidji Gold Processing Plant was constructed, and work began on the Fimiston pit. For the KCGM Super Pit, there was always an eye to public relations.

From the very start of operations within the pit, public viewing was accommodated through the construction of viewing platforms. This was apparently to signify transparency. The first platform was put in position in 1990. In the following year, another processing plant was commissioned, and company engineers developed a long-reach drill, designed for extraction along the deepening wall of the pit. This signified innovation.

In 1991, the Greening the Golden Mile rehabilitation project commenced. This was a very early sign of KCMG's aim to generate a positive public profile for environmentally appropriate production. In 1992, the company invested a further $2 million in this project. This work did not go unnoticed, and the company won the 1995 John Tonkin Greening Award and the Australian Minerals and Energy Environment Foundation Environmental Excellence Award. Three years later, in 1998, the company's Revegetation Centre (Croesus Tree Farm) was announced as the winner of commercial/industrial category of Kalgoorlie–Boulder Garden Beautiful competition.

At the end of their first decade of mining the Super Pit, the

KCGM Super Pit goldmine adjacent to
Kalgoorlie CBD, WA.

company introduced the Komatsu PC8000 shovels. At the time, these were the largest machines of their kind in the world. The economic payoff for such investments become visible in the relative ranking of international gold producers. By 2014, KCGM's operations were ranked fifth largest; by 2020, they ranked second. Currently, KCGM has approximately 1,200 employees and contractors on its payroll. Numerous local businesses are engaged in ongoing projects and supply chains for work by the company.

The hype created about Kalgoorlie is a combination of a sustained narrative of industrial success, coupled with high-impact marketing and promotion, and is undoubtedly linked to the glamour of gold itself.

Such achievements are impressive in many ways, but all the boosting and boasting obscures some of their negative side effects. These include two particular 'spaces of expulsion and indifference'.

'Blasts make floors crack and houses shake'

Williamstown is a suburb of Kalgoorlie located just outside the city's CBD and next to and above KCGM Super Pit. As the pit has grown in width and depth, the work inside the mine has had an increasingly detrimental impact on the lives of those still living in Williamstown. I have used the following description of the suburb's residents as a marker of the challenges these people face in living where they do. They are subject to the effects of blasts within the pit, such as the one I witnessed on my visit to the Super Pit – explosions that are situated at the base and against the wall of the pit closest to Williamstown. In his report about the Williamstown situation, journalist Tom Joyner reported:

> the disturbance caused by regular controlled explosions
> only a few hundred metres beneath them is growing and
> causing damage to property... Lifelong local Fay Henderson
> said after years of fighting, she is exhausted and feels a
> sense of dread that it will not be long before Williamstown
> is gone altogether.

'It's been quite heartbreaking really. It's difficult to feel very uplifted when you think, well maybe tomorrow some other house will go,' she said. 'Williamstown itself is getting smaller and smaller. But I think that it eventually has to pass that we just won't be here, that the mine will engulf us eventually. It's just that it's very hard to be hanging on here, waiting and not knowing what the next step will be.' Blasts make floors crack and houses shake.[3]

Some will write off these outcomes as simply collateral damage from the heavy-duty work of extracting ore from the wealth-generating mine.

Williamstown is a tiny suburb and thus represents only a very small sample of the population of the greater Kalgoorlie–Boulder community. Conversely, it can equally be understood as the home of a large percentage – 21.4 percent – of local senior citizens like Fay Henderson. Census data indicates that it is not a wealthy place, relative to other demographics within WA and Australia more generally. In this sense, the future security of the people living there can be seen as a litmus test about equity and social justice for vulnerable populations vis-à-vis larger demographics and the economic preoccupations of powerful industries and relevant state departments.

Racial strains and injustices

On 29 August 2016, 14-year-old Elijah Doughty died when, riding an allegedly stolen motorbike, he was run over by a man who was pursuing him. Elijah was a member of Kalgoorlie's Indigenous population. The day after his death, hundreds of people protested after the driver was arrested and charged by police. In November 2016, Aboriginal representatives, Kalgoorlie community leaders and state and federal politicians took part in a summit to discuss racial and associated social issues within Kalgoorlie.

After manslaughter charges were processed, local Indigenous people protested outside the courthouse. What became obvi-ous was that Elijah Doughty's death, and the subsequent legal response, was a trigger for the expression of many levels of frustration, including feelings of sustained injustice, prolonged experiences of marginalisation and relative impoverishment. This cocktail of responses was expressed directly in street protest, via some sections of the mass media and through social media outlets.

Inevitably, there was a backlash, much of it online via social media:

> Acting Kalgoorlie Mayor Allan Pendal described the riot as the worst violence he had seen in the town in three decades.
>
> He said it would be naive to suggest there was not a simmering tension between Aboriginal and non-Aboriginal people in the town, but no-one, including the police, expected such a turn of events.
>
> Local MP Wendy Duncan said she had posted a message on Facebook urging people to stop using the social medium to inflame the situation.
>
> 'We cannot have people hiding behind anonymity to say things that are racist, that are inciting people to violence,' she said.
>
> Elijah's grandfather said he hoped some lesson could be learnt from the boy's death.[4]

In 2017, the driver was acquitted of a manslaughter charge and was instead found guilty of dangerous driving causing death. Further protests followed, leading to an elevation of racial tensions within Kalgoorlie. Elsewhere in Australia, rallies of support for Doughty's family and against the trial outcome took place. More recently, following the global Black Lives Matter protests and the #BLM movement, concerns about Doughty's death and the driver's trial have once again risen to the fore

In June 2020, Megan Krakouer and Gerry Georgatos, both involved in suicide prevention programs, published a paper titled, 'Blak lives betrayed – Elijah Doughty'. The paper contains several disturbing contextual issues. They note:

> In the 1967 referendum to amend the Australian Constitution, over 90 percent of Australians who voted supported the amendments to recognise First Australians for inclusion in the Census. However, Kalgoorlie recorded the highest single 'No' vote in any electoral division – 29 percent.
>
> Under eight percent of the Kalgoorlie–Boulder population is Indigenous, but they account for over three quarters of the inmates at the local Eastern Goldfields Regional Prison.
>
> One in five Kalgoorlie–Boulder First Peoples are either in prison or homeless. It is a story of grinding poverty alongside relative affluence, of Blak poverty and white privilege.[5]

There are obvious differences in the quality of homes based on proximity to the mine pit. In summer, houses in the suburbs adjacent to the pit are covered in dust and dirt. As I noted previously, some of these suburbs are subject to significant physical disturbances and associated damage resulting from work within the pit.

Ninga Mia, for example, is a township largely populated by Indigenous people; it is close to Kalgoorlie and the Super Pit. In this respect, Ninga Mia is similar to Parnpajinya near Newman, discussed in the last chapter. Journalists Susan Standen and Tom Joyner noted the following details about Ninga Mia:

> In Ninga Mia, on the doorstep of Australia's largest open-cut gold mine, a WA Government-commissioned audit in 2018 found no major refurbishments had been made to properties since the 1980s.[6]

An audit conducted for a 2020 KPMG report found that people in this community were living in houses unfit for habitation.[7] Standen and Joyner commented:

> These mines (the Super Pit & Whaleback) produce millions of dollars in gold and iron ore each year, contributing to the prosperity of Australia with jobs and investment.

> But those living in these Aboriginal communities see none of that wealth, and instead live in wretched conditions without basic amenities such as a landline telephone and internet, and with constant plumbing issues.[8]

It's now over 50 years since Bill Stanner's Boyer Lectures described the 'cult of forgetfulness practised on a national scale', a national characteristic indicative of 'The Great Australian Silence'. The prelude to, and aftermath of, Elijah Doughty's death are marked not by silence but by subversive online commentary. I have named some of these enduring social and racial issues that are being lived out on the margins of both Kalgoorlie and Newman. For all the excitement and hype about the wealth being generated by both massive mines, there are other realities that need to be acknowledged and rectified.

What future?

The final issue about Kalgoorlie as a mining centre surrounds the question of what is its future when gold mining ends? The sale of their respective shares in the mine by Newmont Goldcorp and Barrick Gold signals this as a possibility.

Conversely, an announcement about plans to establish a cracking and leaching plant for rare earth materials possibly opens a new chapter in the already long-term story of the city and the rest of Australia.

Lynas Corporation specialises in mining, processing and distributing rare earth minerals. The company currently mines ore from its Central Lanthanide Deposit at Mount Weld, approximately 400 km north-east of Kalgoorlie.[9] Currently, the ore is shipped from Fremantle to Malaysia for processing. Over several years, Malaysian activists have protested about the low-level radiation produced in this process. Their concerns seem unheard; Lynas Corporation is currently building a Rare

Earths Processing plant in Kalgoorlie. At this facility, material mined at Mt Weld will undergo initial processing before being transported to Malaysia or the USA. This is another example of material mined in Australia becoming one part of an extended supply chain involving extraction, processing and refining before entry into the global marketplace of commodities.

Post-demolition wreckage of the former
Anglesea Power Station, Victoria

10.

Closure and rehabilitation: Anglesea Mine

The land of the Wathaurong language group

On 3 October 2018, the power station in the Anglesea power facility was demolished. The photo on the previous page of a tangled mess of steel and other building material sets the scene for a narrative about what is to be done and what can be made possible in the rehabilitation phase of an abandoned mining facility. The image offers a warrant for considering the need for posing 'What's next?' and 'What's possible?' questions.

Establishing the mine

In 1961, work began at Alcoa's Point Henry site, in Corio Bay, Victoria, on a plant for smelting and semi fabricating aluminium. Two years later, ingots were produced and shipped from the site. In 1965, a rolling mill went into production. In 1968, the Anglesea Coal Mine opened. Located 40 km southwest of Geelong, the mine produced brown coal as a fuel to heat the power station's boilers. The following year, 1969, the power station began generating electricity for transmission to the Point Henry plant.

By the early 2000s, Alcoa's Point Henry plant was producing and selling ingots and rolled aluminium worth hundreds of millions of dollars. However, the company was also flagging concerns about the high costs of production, relative to the falling prices for aluminium products. The company raised questions about the medium-to-long-term viability of the aging plant.

Closing the mine

In early 2014, Alcoa announced its decision to close the Point Henry smelter. By the end of that year, all operations had ceased. The plant and its mine closed at least four decades earlier than Alcoa had originally planned. Apart from a smelter at Portland in the west of Victoria, Alcoa's only remaining sites in Australia are in WA.

Mine and production plant closures represent a hard reality for local people. The flow on effects were predictable. Over 80 employees lost work. Local traders, who had supplied the mine and power plant's workers and managers, lost an important source of income. This also happened in Morwell, with the closure of the Hazelwood plant, and in countless other places. Much of everyday life comes to an end.

How are such endings handled? Firstly, this involves the pragmatics of the ending. At Morwell/Hazelwood, workers symbolically left their hard hats hanging on the wire structures of gates and fences at the entrance. On the grander stage, what happens to the decommissioned, superfluous physical plant? At Morwell/Hazelwood, the destruction of the eight chimneys of the power station and then the central buildings became a major spectacle, watched from safe viewing locations. The actual moments the chimneys collapsed was a tailor-made dramatic event widely covered by the mass media.

Endings involve the hype of formal announcements and the associated media representations of the key moments. Then, behind the scenes, are the legal issues associated with closure and termination arrangements and agreements. But there is always anguish, loss and confusion about the future for those left behind.

If things go well, there are the pragmatics of rehabilitation for the agent without a voice: the land that will remain long after mining has ceased. But how healthy will it remain?

In the area immediately adjacent to the Anglesea township, the closure also had an impact on local wildlife and marine life in waterways flowing into Bass Strait. An impact statement prepared and distributed by the Victorian Government graphically describes the scope of these changes:

The closure of the Anglesea mine exposes the community and environment to a number of changes, some site related and many stemming from the positive role mine water discharge had in maintaining water flows in a hydrological system with declining natural water flows. The absence of mine related water discharges of 4.5 million litres per day will bring many hydrological changes, with longer-term environmental impacts expected from (1) acid sulphate soils, (2) a reduction of water flowing into the Anglesea River with subsequent drop in river and estuary levels, (3) an increase in heavy metals concentrations and (4) drying out of marshes with further acidic effects. These are expected to alter vegetation communities, increase the risk of algal blooms and reduce water habitat and seagrass areas, all with flow on effects on ecological processes. Active intervention with on-going pumping of water and runoff buffering will be required to protect the sensitive river and estuarine dependent ecosystems from deleterious change.

This commentary highlights a series of issues that have not been adequately addressed when mines close. It points to some of the anticipated geophysical consequences of the mine's closure, especially about the marshland, where the water for the mine has been extracted, and the downstream impact on water flows along the watercourse of the Anglesea River and then into Bass Strait beyond.

This issue has direct relevance for the management of the open-cut pit in Morwell. In early June 2022, Environment Victoria posted a bulletin about this matter:

The mine that fuelled Hazelwood power station is bigger than Melbourne CBD and cleaning it up will be the largest rehabilitation project our state has seen. It will also set a precedent for the remaining mines in the Valley. With the rehabilitation plans undergoing an Environment Effects

Statement (EES) process later this year it's our chance to get rehabilitation right.[1]

Friends of Latrobe Water and Environment Victoria organised a forum to consider the massive amount of work required to clean up the coal pit and to carefully monitor the downstream effects on water use.[2]

In countless examples across the nation, such rehabilitation work is conducted after the fact and without due consideration of the longer-term environmental effects of closures.

Texas, Queensland

Texas is a Queensland town on the border with NSW. In 2015, ABC investigative journalists documented farmers' concerns that cyanide from an abandoned silver mine could flow into local streams that feed into the massive Murray–Darling River system. Highly polluted water was filtering into the system, with highly damaging environmental consequences.

In early 2016, Steven Miles, Queensland Minister for Environment and Heritage Protection for National Parks and the Great Barrier Reef, announced that the Queensland Government had begun taking a direct and active role in the long-term management of mine sites:

> The Queensland Government has introduced a bill to Parliament to ensure that in future mine operators can't simply walk away from their responsibilities if they choose to shut down their operations, such as has happened here in Texas... If passed, the Environmental Protection (Chain of Responsibility) Amendment Bill will provide stronger laws to deal with the issue of businesses leaving Queensland taxpayers with costly environmental clean-up bills.[3]

The Amended Act came into effect on 27 April 2016.

A subsequent Queensland Government announcement provided useful details about the history and purpose of the Act. These details highlight the fact that, over the past decade in Australia, there have many legislative changes seeking to address problems associated with abandoned mines. The intent of this legislation is captured by the phrase 'chain of responsibility'. The Queensland Government intended to:

> expand the powers of the Department of Environment
> and Science to ensure that companies and their related
> parties bear the cost of managing and rehabilitating sites
> and prevent leaving the Queensland taxpayers with costly
> environmental clean-up bills.[4]

This signifies that there are now formal and legal steps being taken to address the issues associated with the long-term effects of mining. In a follow-up bulletin about Queensland's legislation, the ABC's Mark Willacy commented:

> Queensland alone has more than 15,000 abandoned mines,
> including 300 classified as mega, large or medium size. A
> report on these mines by the environmental group Lock
> the Gate Alliance is recommending the introduction of an
> independent authority to rehabilitate the sites.[5]

Anglesea's future

Through material accessed under Freedom of Information, Environment Victoria sourced a series of guidelines that had been submitted for the closure and rehabilitation of the Anglesea site. Three statements from that list are worth noting:

> Alcoa's current objective for site rehabilitation is to establish
> a diverse, self-sustaining healthy woodland ecosystem that
> maintains or enhances the surrounding land use such as
> conservation, recreation and natural values (p. 57).

> Alcoa notes that their responsibility for the site should not
> cease until the stability of the works and the regenerative
> capacity of the ecosystem has been demonstrated (p. 145).
> Alcoa notes the importance of understanding current closure

and decommissioning costs, in the event of unexpected closure (p. 150).[6]

A summative statement by Environment Victoria is significant:

> Alcoa seems to be taking their closure responsibilities
> seriously, which is encouraging, and there are details
> in their Work Plan that seem to be largely absent from
> corresponding documents for the Latrobe Valley mines.

The theme of environmental responsibility is clearly fore-grounded here. While rehabilitation work in the Latrobe Valley does not fare well, what is happening at Anglesea is viewed positively.

A year after the closure, Alcoa and the Eden Project (UK) announced a proposal to develop the mine site according to a model used in a project in England: an abandoned mine pit in Cornwall had become an award-winning education centre. One of the Eden Project's co-founders, Tim Smit, provided the ratio-nale behind this idea:

> In the beginning the idea was very simple – let's take a
> place of utter dereliction and create life in it... We are an
> educational charity and social enterprise. Our global mission
> is to create a movement that builds relationships between
> people and the natural world to demonstrate the power of
> working together for the benefit of all living things.[7]

This statement seems applicable to Hazelwood and Anglesea power stations after their destruction. Smit's use of the words 'utter dereliction' is part of the reason I began this chapter with the photograph of the wreckage of the Anglesea Power station. This photograph, and others that I took after the Hazelwood power station and its chimneys were destroyed, certainly signify that dramatic changes are occurring. But matters of rehabilitation processes remain – what is needed to restore, rehabilitate and regenerate environments damaged by mining.

I began this book with an account of a fire in the mine pit at Morwell and the closure of the Hazelwood power station. In that case, the mine was located adjacent to a small community in a regional location in a southern hemisphere country. But that mine and that fire were part of an extended global assemblage. The owner of the mine and power station, ENGIE, a multinational company based in Paris, had acquired market-based property rights to make decisions that would have profound effects on a community located across the world. This separation and significant power differential make the concept of a chain of responsibility so important. There is much to learn from what is happening with the rehabilitation process underway at Anglesea.

In the Anglesea situation, Alcoa is a large, corporate aluminium producer based in the USA. The parallels here are instructive. The financial control and decision-making power base is located far from the material site of production. The labour force of workers at the plant is largely comprised of local people. The physical consequences of both the Anglesea and the Hazelwood power stations are experienced locally. The subsequent clean up necessitates being alert to the flow on effects in the local environment, including air quality, residues in plants and topsoil nearby and impact on local watercourses.

Living only 16 km from the Anglesea Mine site, I have visited the mine pit many times during rehabilitation. From a lookout on the northern side of the mine, I have watched large graders and earth-moving trucks reconstructing the edges of the southern and western escarpments. I have noted the effect of planting of native grasses in that same area. Currently, at the end of a wet winter and spring, the growth appears lush and healthy. I have also observed extensive work in water management, involving drain construction around the edge of the lake that is currently forming at the bottom of the basin.

The project underway in Anglesea has the potential to offer lessons in the pragmatics of completing rehabilitation work and to provide guidelines for future mining projects about embedding funding for rehabilitation into every mining enterprise at the start. That would make the rehabilitation of the site, post-closure, a central part of the purchase, planning, production and postproduction procedures of all future mining projects. Indeed, government permits should make this compulsory and enforceable.

Wildflowers located in land being rehabilitated in the former Anglesea brown coal mine, Victoria

PART FOUR

Spaces in Between

The further I travelled, the more I become aware of many other issues associated with land ownership, land use and land rights. Some related directly to mining, others indirectly. These became evident in the spaces in between my main locations.

11.
Life in remote regions

Most Australians live far away from the sights, sounds and effects of mining on various scales. Remote and very remote locations are out of sight and probably out of mind. As I drove between the mining locations of this study, I realised that the spaces between them should not be out of mind. To deeply understand the many worlds of mining and the related practices of land use, we need to move beyond metro-centric and coastal-centric perspectives.

A high proportion Australia's population is concentrated in two widely separated coastal regions – the south-east and east, and the south-west. Of the two regions, the south-east and east is by far the largest, both in area and in population.

The Australian Bureau of Statistics (ABS) notes that 89 percent of the population live in urban environments, and 82 percent live 'close' to the coast. Australia's population was 25,750,198 at 30 September 2021. Of this total, 18,586,000 people lived in major cities, which amounts to 72 percent of the total population. In contrast, 26 percent live in inner and outer regional Australia, with the remainder living in remote and very remote areas. As of 30 June 2020:

- 4,557,000 people lived in Inner Regional Australia.
- 2,063,000 people lived in Outer Regional Australia.
- 291,000 people lived in Remote Australia.
- 201,000 people lived in Very Remote Australia.[1]

In straightforward, pragmatic terms, my trip from Broken Hill to the next mine site, Roxby Downs, was a very long drive that would stretch out over several days. When I originally chose my target destinations, I was primarily interested in visiting places where different forms of material were mined. Roxby Downs interested me because of its status and controversial history as a producer of uranium. The Argyle mine was interesting because it was a site for the extraction of diamonds, one of the few such locations in Australia. After making these choices, I simply put in place an itinerary that involved travel between sites. The distance between the two places meant approximately 3,000 km of road travel.

What I had overlooked in organising my trip, in this stripped-down, nuts-and-bolts approach of getting from place to place, was the impact of experiencing travel into and through places that were very different to the urban locales in which I have spent most of my life. Departure from Roxby Downs marked the point at which my experiences of such differences moved to a new level.

I had a choice of routes. The first option involved driving on a dirt track – the Borefield Road – north from Roxby Dam Village to link with another gravel road – the Oodnadatta Track – that would take me back to the Stuart Highway at Marla, a tiny settlement 235 km north of Coober Pedy. The positive side of this option was a drive through genuine outback territory, passing close to the southern edge of the fabled Lake Eyre. The negative side involved the weather. With the prospect of showers throughout the region, I could get trapped on a road that turned to mud and encounter floods spreading across the track. Option two involved driving back south on the sealed road, through Woomera, to link up again with the Stuart Highway. Apart from the added security of being on a sealed road, this route took me through the opal mining town of Coober Pedy – not one of my chosen mine locations, but suddenly a bonus addition to my sites list. I chose the second option.

Another issue is embedded in this little anecdote about choice and decision. It speaks to a further dimension of my ongoing education involving the push–pull psychology of my personal comfort levels. The first option – along the unsealed roads through the outback – while attractive, involved some risk of complications and the possibility of getting held up by pushing into the unknown. The second option – back along the Stuart Highway and through Coober Pedy – was relatively secure.

Little places and mining histories

In remote Australia, dotted along the highways, many small communities have played some sort of role in the world of mining. Some were quick stopover places, allowing mining people to rest and refuel on their way to somewhere else. Others, at one time or another, were part of the extended supply chain that took raw materials from the mines onto the sites of processing, production and distribution. Yet more little communities grew around such places, partly to service them. These places were often connected to each other; sometimes mining provided the connecting tissue. They are usually a forgotten part of the story of mining, as are the stories about their survival after the miners departed.

Major mining locations have many connections to elsewhere – to businesses, transport systems, emergency services and government agencies. Places and institutions beyond them depend on them. When owners or governments, often from a considerable distance away, make major strategic decisions about mining, the effects ripple outwards to many other parts of the wider region. This point also applies to the smaller mining locations of the gold rush era. When the gold was gone, so were the miners. These places once mattered to mining but were abandoned when they ran out of desirable extractable minerals.

I passed through many such places. Some seemed to be thriving, others barely surviving. Changes in mining had changed them. I wondered what else kept them going. I wondered what people in these places now do for a living, how they spend their time and what they do for company.

I left Broken Hill and drove south-west on the Barrier Highway, humming 'Hit the road, Jack', which had become a personal departure anthem. The first couple of lines of the Ray Charles classic include the directive, 'and don't you come back no more, no more.' I drove away from Broken Hill feeling that the words were apt. I doubted I would have the time or reason for returning; but then again, I thought to myself, 'Who knows what is in store next?'

A few kilometres out of the city, I drove through sparsely vegetated, very flat terrain. The drive was easy, the road surface excellent, and cars or trucks scarce. I switched on cruise control and settled into a comfortable driver zone that I rarely experience in the city. It took no time at all to reach the state border, cross into SA and pass through the small town of Cockburn.

In the 2021 National Census, Cockburn was listed with a population of 12 residents. Subsequent research showed that this town once had an important role in the transportation of locally mined ore to Port Pirie (SA) for smelting. It was part of mining's extended supply chains, one of a range of places that provide key links.

Nearby is the small town of Silverton, in the south-west of NSW; it lies approximately 25 kms west of Broken Hill, 1,180 kms from Sydney, and 550 kms from Adelaide. In the 2021 National Census, Silverton was listed with a population of 48 people.

In the 1870s, discovery of a reef of silver led to the establishment of a mine. As would happen with metals extracted at Broken Hill, the minerals needed to be transported to a smelter constructed at Port Pirie, 400 kms away in SA, on the eastern shoreline of Spencer Gulf.

This process of transportation was complicated because NSW and SA had different gauge rail lines. To deal with this problem, Cockburn became an interchange point where ore, transported by rail from Silverton and Broken Hill, was transferred to SA trains travelling to and from Port Pirie. For over 80 years, Cockburn was an important railway interchange site. This arrangement continued until 1970. Currently, the only visible sign of this rail transporting process is a large, elevated water tank, once used by the trains, but now acting as a source of water in case of local wildfires.

Slow time

If you attend to it, there is a very different sense of time in the outback and outer regions. Time seems to slow down and make way for other things, other thoughts. The senses are intensified, and small moments are magnified.

I had the cruise control set at a tad over 100 km per hour, so I was travelling almost 10 km under the legal speed limit. A glance in the rear vision mirror showed that a convoy of four sedans was about to catch and overtake me; but we entered some low hills, bends in the road and double lines.

For a short time, I was the lead vehicle in the line-up, made anxious by the way the four cars behind me were bunched, obviously strategically placed to pass me at the first opportunity. As we moved out of the hills and back onto the flat open plain, the cars whizzed past. I noticed that each driver was female and most of the passengers were kids, so this must be an expedition outside school hours. Their time was clearly so precious to them that this space needed to be compressed by speed. In the blink of an eye, I was once again the only car crossing this vast, empty space.

I quickly passed through Mingary and Olary, two other small towns on this stretch of highway, and decided to stop at the next place with a store. When I pulled up in a tiny place named Manna Hill, I was thirsty and seeking mineral water. As I approached the store, I noticed an elderly woman walking, ever so slowly, along a road that ran perpendicular to the store. She had her head down, and each step seemed to take a great deal of effort. She appeared to be coming in this direction; but, at the pace she was moving, her arrival would be some time off.

I entered a poorly lit space and hesitated while my eyes adjusted to the change of conditions. A woman behind the counter acknowledged my arrival with a nod. Looking around, I immediately noticed that the store contained an absolutely minimal amount of stock on the counter and shelves, but it was displayed with neatness and order.

While I was deliberating about my drink choice, the woman recommended the cola-based drink. She considered it one of the best drinks she had ever tasted. I replied that I would take her advice to see what I thought about it. 'You will have to tell me what you think when you come back here!' she declared. I decided not to mention the Ray Charles-inspired message to myself.

As I was about to leave the store, the old woman I'd seen earlier on the street reached the door. The woman behind the counter greeted her with great animation and volume.

'Hello Ivy, what are you up to?' she asked.

'I've come to see you and have a chat,' came Ivy's reply. Immediately, both women broke into laughter. As I reached my car, I could hear that the chat was already underway – good company in a shop where the staff member has time to keep things tidy and to notice the hesitation of a stranger about their choice of drink.

Manna Hill was once just a location on a stock route. This changed in the late 1880s, when a railway line was established. It then became a 'water supply and maintenance point' as well as a route to the Mannahill Goldfields. At that time, the government of the colony sought to encourage gold mining by providing financial incentives. These, many nearby discoveries and the railway line helped fuel a goldrush to Mannahill Goldfields and other adjacent sites. Gold mining in the area was 'characterised by a series of short periods of high gold production as large numbers of men rushed to, and quickly exhausted, each new find'.[2] Mineral discoveries led to regular and rapid population movement. While highly populated and productive at their peak, Mannahill Goldfields were virtually deserted by 1889. An 1886 article from the Melbourne-based *Argus* described the route and location:

> The journey is principally across saltbush plains and low undulating hills, lightly timbered with mulga and ti-tree. Water and food on the road are both scarce and of inferior quality. The distance from Adelaide to Petersburg (now Peterborough) is 150 miles. The first train leaves Adelaide about 8 o'clock in the morning and reaches Petersburg at 3pm. A second train leaves Adelaide shortly before 5 in the evening, but only goes as far as Terowie 10 miles from Petersburg, reaching Terowie at midnight. There is one train a day from Petersburg to Mannahill. This journey covers a distance of between 80 and 90 miles, over flat uninteresting country. Provision has to

be made by travellers for their own refreshments until Mannahill is reached. Here there is a large hotel, capable of accommodating about 50 people. In shearing time the proprietor does a fair trade, shearers and teamsters from the surrounding stations being the principal customers. The country around here possesses a very dreary outlook.[3]

No city-based newspaper is likely to cover Manna Hill these days. It is largely seen as just a stopover place, for pastoralists and travellers, on the Barrier Highway and Indian–Pacific railway line. But for some it is home – a good place for good chat.

12.

Terra nullius mindsets

An extractivist mindset has different components. Klein has helped us understand this, and I have offered many examples. A key component in Australia is the notion of *terra nullius*. For mining, the empty land is only useful for what can be extracted from it and turned into profit. It can be exploited, then abandoned. According to this logic, the 'barren and unpopulated' outback can be utilised for any purpose, without concern for damage to human and non-human life and without fear of repercussions. Colonisation led the way in the application of this *terra nullius* mindset. But mining also subscribes to and normalises it. This mindset, I contend, carries over into other spheres of activity and institutions, including government. Beauty, silence and the temporal imagination are all antithetical to the *terra nullius* mindset.

Late in the afternoon of Friday 24 July, I was driving on Highway A87 headed for Coober Pedy, an opal mining location 800 km north of Adelaide. This was bona fide remote territory.

Increasingly aware that I was not giving full attention to the road ahead, I slowed my vehicle before stopping in a suitable space. Driver fatigue was not the issue. Distracted by curiosity and a growing feeling of excitement, I had been scanning the landscape from the extremities of my visual range, left to right. In so doing, I had been paying minimal attention to the road. Standing outside the vehicle, I took a moment to stretch. I turned and absorbed the spectacle that was the 360° of landscape and the far distant horizon. I was awestruck.

In the soft pre-dusk light, I became acutely aware that, apart from the sealed road, I was standing in a vast space that appeared endless and free of any structures created by humans. Around and beyond me, as far as my eyes could see, I saw the relatively flat ground of a gibber plain covered by orange-brown stones and green-grey saltbush. At the outer limits of my vision, where earth and sky met, the dramatic and vibrant colours of the evening sky fused with the muted shades of the landscape.

I felt as if I had been transported into a Terence Malick movie that was dramatising the full sensory wonders and feelings of the day's 'magic hour'. I am referring specifically to Malick's *Days of Heaven*, a film that included many poetic images of vast expanses of land, filmed in soft, fading light in the open plains of Alberta (Canada). The film has been described as perhaps the most pictorially beautiful depiction of the Great Plains ever created on film. In this moment, art and life fused in an experience I can only describe as wondrous.

Paradoxically, the silence amplified these sensations. There was no road noise of other vehicles, no sound of electronic devices, no planes passing overhead, no people talking, dogs barking or birds calling. It appeared that I was standing within a vast, ancient, natural amphitheatre.

Stimulated by the uniqueness of the moment, I found myself imagining groups of Indigenous people slowly crossing the plains – as they have done for many thousands of years. I imagined early European explorers traversing the land with horses, and Afghan camel-traders transporting goods. It occurred to me that, although the racial and cultural identity of the humans travelling across this land has expanded over time, the physical environment may have changed little.

This felt like a place where time was measured in multiples of millennia.

I did not see my surrounds as barren, as devoid of life, vitality and meaning. Instead, I saw a vast open region with a long biophysical history in which life exists in forms not readily apparent.

My experience and celebration of being in this time and place was short lived. Feelings of mental dissonance soon crept in as I began to recalibrate exactly where I was standing. The location was the Stuart Highway, approximately 50 km south of Coober Pedy, a small opal mining and tourist town in northern SA, 450 km north-west of Adelaide.

Seclusion and secrecy

I was on a section of highway that provided a public thoroughfare through a restricted zone known as the Woomera Range Complex. An explanation about the nature of this 'facility', provided on a noticeboard in the town of Woomera, read:

> WELCOME TO THE WORLD'S LARGEST TEST & EVALUATION RANGE
>
> Strategic Role: The RAAF Woomera Test Range (WTR) is a highly specialised test and evaluation capability supporting both Defence and wider National objectives.
>
> Ground Area and Airspace: The Woomera Prohibited Area (WPA) defines the Range's ground area and covers 127,000 sq km (49 sq mls) or an area roughly the size of England or the US state of Florida.

In the postwar years of the late 1940s, the vast open space of this arid region, unused for farming or other industry and devoid of permanent human settlements (although not of nomadic peoples), was identified as suitable for weapons testing. The Australian Government of the time gave the British Government permission to conduct nuclear weapons tests and trials of long-range rockets. The highly contentious and secretive use of this massive area is signified by the language used on the noticeboard: 'highly specialised test and evaluation capability'.

The federal and state governments hold a constitutional right to excise large swathes of territory, as has occurred with the Woomera Range Complex (WRC), and to license access to minerals and other resources, such as water from artesian aquifers deep underground. These rights and licences and associated political developments have profound effects on the lives and wellbeing of groups of traditional Indigenous owners and custodians of the land. The story of nuclear weapons tests during the 1950s and early 1960s illustrates the seriousness of this matter.

Australia – nuclear test site

In 1952, the Australian Government had signed a contract with the Combined Development Agency, representing the UK and USA, to supply uranium.[1] At the same time, in a remarkable expression of executive power, the pro-royalist Prime Minister of Australia, Robert Menzies, agreed to a British request to begin testing atomic weapons in its former colony.[2] At the dawn of the Cold War nuclear arms race, Australia was an active participant at both ends of the weapons cycle: as the source of the primary fuel and as the testing ground.

British tests began in 1952 and concluded in 1963. During this time, Britain exploded 12 bombs, the largest being 60 kilotons (1 kiloton = 1,000 tons of TNT). They tested three devices at Montebello Islands, off the coast of WA, and nine on the Australian mainland in SA. The tests were conducted in clusters and codenamed as Operations 'Hurricane', 'Totem', 'Mosaic', 'Buffalo' and 'Antler'.[3] Within this same timeframe, literally hundreds of 'minor trials' of associated weapon devices also took place. Several of these tests involved deadly plutonium as the material source and occurred during the period of the USA–Soviet Union moratorium on nuclear testing. These so-called 'minor trials' were categorised with innocuous titles such as 'Kittens', 'Rats', 'Vixen' and 'Tims'.[4]

The British Government conducted these major and minor tests under a veil of extreme control and secrecy and has not released some of the information about the processes and outcomes of the tests even now; finding and publicising the cold, hard facts about what occurred has been an extended and problematic process.

In the decade and a half after the tests, increasing numbers of people who had been involved became ill, and their medical conditions became known. Information about what had occurred began to filter into the public domain. Displaced Indigenous landowners of the Pitjantjatjara people of the Anangu groups of the north-west of SA shared stories and anecdotes, which began to enter the wider community.

Decisions about the repair and restoration of the test sites were necessary, and so more information became public. Concerns about the truth of what had occurred grew and began to consolidate into a chorus of protest. In 1980, the government of the time was pressured into establishing an inquiry to satisfy demands for an alternative and more detailed account of the political and cultural facts of the testing period. The Australian Ionising Radiation Advisory Council was commissioned to conduct the inquiry and delivered a report three years later.[5] This report is widely considered a 'whitewash'; it basically confirmed and legitimised the pre-existing, superficial narratives about the testing program.[6]

It required a change of government in late 1983 to begin to lift the veil of secrecy concealing the facts and consequences of these events. In July 1984, a Royal Commission was established and directed to investigate many matters, including the nature of measurements taken during and after testing, health warnings provided to those involved, safety procedures used to control movement of persons in the testing area, fallout measurements and monitoring, disposal of contaminated material and the content of reports and other classified documentation held by the British Government.[7]

This project, steeped in secrecy and careless of the safety and wellbeing of the local Indigenous populations, took place during the 1950s and early 1960s Cold War era. Subsequently, from 1969 to 1999, Australia and the USA jointly operated the Nurrungar Joint Defence Facility, a ground-based listening station designed to monitor space-based surveillance.

This militarised and cold war narrative doesn't capture the full history of the government's use of this remote region. Between late 1999 and early 2003, the geographic remoteness and isolation was deemed suitable for the construction of a detention centre to imprison so-called 'unauthorised' arrivals – more correctly, refugees.

The facility then became the Woomera Immigration Reception and Processing Centre (WIRPC), 'housing' over 1,400 people in 2001. During the three and half years of its operation, the WIRPC saw several episodes of resistance, protest and conflict by detainees and outside protestors.

Subsequently, the centre featured in media reports, nationally and internationally. The United Nations Refugee Agency and the Commissioner for Human Rights scrutinised it and asserted that the conditions represented 'an additional ordeal' for those housed there. Following the centre's closure, the Woomera facility, now the WRC, once again became used for national defence purposes.

Under the banner of *terra nullius*, governments, military leaders and policymakers had deemed this region a space for military and security purposes, including the testing of atomic weapons and, more recently, the internment of so-called illegal arrivals.

In short, in the more recent narrative associated with this extended region, the land is deemed useful for bombing, weapons testing and the harsh treatment of those deemed as alien, threatening and potentially dangerous. It is also deemed uninhabited, despite the presence of Indigenous people. According to the *terra nullius* mindset, because this land is so remote, it can be used and abused by governments as a hiding place and dumping ground.

But this vast region is now implicated in a national narrative of secrecy and shame. As details about the secret testing were made public, it became clear that Australia was still regarded as a colony by Britain. This program of testing weapons and researching the effects of radiation fallout on Australian servicemen positioned Australia as subordinate and subservient.

But the colonial *terra nullius* mindset is most evident in the treatment of Indigenous people. Nine of the tests took place in and around the homelands of the Indigenous peoples of the region – homelands they hold sacred. To those with a *terra nullius* mindset, no land is sacred.

13.

Wounded land

Following my roadside stop and photo shoot on the gibber plain, I drove along the Stuart Highway to Coober Pedy. This is a very isolated, sparsely populated region. According to the Australian Statistical Geography Standard, I was deep within a very remote part of the country. This classification has helped to reinforce a dominant view that, demographically, Australia is an urban and coastal nation but with massive areas of 'nothingness' or, more dramatically, 'terra nullius'.

The *terra nullius* mindset discussed in Chapter 12 acts to extinguish the stories and lived experiences of legions of current and former generations of Indigenous groupings. It is thus appropriate and necessary that I acknowledge that, during this part of my travel, I was passing through Arabana land, with Kokata land to the west and Wankanguru land to the east.

My subsequent research about this region and its traditional owners revealed that the tribal name is Ngurabanna. It refers to water holes, known as mound springs, that are vital water sources in this very arid area. Arabana is the name of the distinctive Sturt desert pea flower.[1]

Importantly, Arabana Native Title had been declared in 2012, providing legal recognition of the ownership of 69,000 square kms by the Arabana Aboriginal Corporation Inc. This is the largest area of Native Title in Australia. Its size speaks volumes about the current custodians and those who carried its legacy over such a long time.

This complex custodial relationship illustrates an intimate form of interconnection that embraces many different levels of meaning and practice. Ambelin Kwaymullina, a Palyku woman, clarifies this complexity:

> For Aboriginal peoples, country is much more than a place. Rock, tree, river, hill, animal, human – all were formed of the same substance by the Ancestors who continue to live in land, water, sky. Country is filled with relations speaking language and following Law, no matter whether the shape of that relation is human, rock, crow, wattle. Country is loved, needed, and cared for, and country loves, needs, and cares for her peoples in turn. Country is family, culture, identity. Country is self.[2]

I saw no such relationship in Coober Pedy.

Coober Pedy: 'Opals Capital of the World'

Late in the day, and in fading light, I drove to Coober Pedy. I had identified an underground motel as my day's resting place. After booking in, I chatted with the father of the woman who owned the motel. Our talk was a bonus; he gave me a no-holds-barred commentary about the town and its history of opal mining. He had lived in the area for over 40 years and told me about his time working underground and about the lure of a rich load of ore. He then gave me his frank assessment – that the work back then was very 'tough and too hard for most people now.'

I was in no doubt about the harshness of the place as a work site. Weather recordings regularly measure summer temperatures above 45° C, dust and sandstorms are common, and the annual rainfall average is only 175 mm. Not surprisingly, many residents live and work underground. My room in the motel was a compact cavern, dug into the side of the sandstone hill. It was clean, neat, comfortable and quiet. In the hot, dry and dusty extremes at the height of summer, this accommodation would offer very liveable conditions.

During my initial wander through Coober Pedy, I came across many stores selling opals. The trade in opals is the distinguishing retail feature of this small town. Later, from the motel perched on the hill just beyond the small CBD, I had an excellent view of shops and houses, and more indications that this was a mining location.

Across the landscape were many different signs of a small-scale extractive industry: machines parked in streets and on vacant land; trucks of all sizes; metal apparatus protruding from mullock heaps. The countless metal pipes poking out of the ground provided ventilation for underground workspaces, homes and caverns like my motel room. I mused about the people who, over many years, have been lured to Coober Pedy by the hope that they will find opal – the beautiful gemstones.

Some opals are expensive and precious; others are cheaper and more common. The *opalsdownunder* website explains:

> Body tone is one of the most important factors in the
> classification and valuation of opals. Body tone refers to the
> background or the 'underlying colour' of the opal, which
> ranges from black through dark to light. Generally, opals
> with a black or dark body tone are more valuable than those
> with a white, light, or crystal body tone, because a stone with
> a darker body tone tends to display colours more vibrantly.[3]

Eventually, they will be cut, polished and turned into jewellery. The range means that they can cater to various markets.

From an industrial and labour perspective, opal can be extracted economically through small-scale operations. Miners buy permits and then work for themselves. They regard being self-employed and running their own agenda as an attractive feature of opal prospecting and mining. The capacity for hard work, in harsh conditions, is considered testimony to a rugged outback form of masculinity.

The District Council website calls Cooper Pedy the 'Opals Capital of the World'. But it also points to some recent changes in the town.

Over the last 10–20 years, a drop in prospecting activity and a decline in the number of active miners have affected the health of the mining industry. In recent times, the continuing

Mullock heaps adjacent to Coober Pedy houses, SA

development of Coober Pedy now depends more on the increasingly important role of tourism to and through the town and its recognition as a major regional centre for the outback.

At first glance, Coober Pedy looked less like a tourist destination than a heavily scarred and damaged environment. Many mullock heaps – discarded dirt, rock and rubble – are piled in spaces away from the centre of the town. Strewn across this jumble of hillocks were numerous bits and pieces of broken and discarded mining equipment and associated aging machinery. It typified many locations where mining operations leave an ugly legacy on the land. It made me think of the mining notion of overburden.

Overburden (also called waste or spoil) is the material such as the rock, soil and ecosystem that lies above an area that lends itself to economic exploitation.

During my time in Coober Pedy, I was both fascinated and disturbed by the sight of these large areas of mullock heaps. I can see that other visitors and tourists might find this moonscape vista interesting – along with the novelty of human life underground and the many opportunities to purchase locally mined opals. But I also see the irony, that the disturbed land helps to sell Coober Pedy as an interesting and distinctive tourist location.

The NT Intervention

Having rested, wandered, restocked and revived, I was ready to move north, across the state border and into the NT on my way to Alice Springs.

The NT is an area that was, and still is, subject to federal government interventions – processes and programs designed to impose and maintain strict controls over many aspects of life for people in Indigenous communities. In 2007, the federal Coalition government introduced a set of procedures titled 'Northern Territory Emergency Response (NTER)'.

The NTER was triggered by the widespread response to the publication of the *Little Children are Sacred* report, a document advocating for the protection of Indigenous children from sexual abuse. This intervention, made public by Prime Minister John Howard and Minister for Families and Community Services and Indigenous Affairs Mal Brough, was supposedly:

> In response to the national emergency confronting the welfare of Aboriginal children in the Northern Territory... prompting the Australian Government to implement... immediate, broad ranging measures to stabilise and protect communities in the crisis area.[4]

The Intervention imposed many restrictions and checks: access to, and use of, alcohol; school attendance checks; health checks; supervision over living conditions in communities and camps; intensified policing strategies; and income management of welfare and income support payments.[5]

When the NT Government hesitated in effecting these instructions, the federal government quickly intervened in a move designed in three phases, summarised as an intent to 'stabilise, normalise and then exit' from the situation.

This pre-emptive approach was taken to an unprecedented level when personnel from the Australian Defence Force and the Australian Federal Police were engaged to supervise the so-called stabilisation and normalisation. Ruthless policing and surveillance were involved. The carceral State was in full swing.

Subsequent governments from both major parties have maintained and varied the legislation and its range of measures:
- removing the permit system for access to Aboriginal land
- abolishing government-funded Community Development Employment Projects
- subjecting Aboriginal children to teaching in a language they don't speak for the first four hours at school
- quarantining 50 percent of welfare payments
- suspending the Racial Discrimination Act
- expecting Aboriginal people to lease property to the government in return for basic services
- compulsorily acquiring Aboriginal land

- conducting mandatory health checks on Aboriginal children without consulting their parents.

Multiple layers of shocking contradiction are evident in the measures listed above. A prime example is that, collectively, they clearly contravene provisions in the Commonwealth *Racial Discrimination Act 1975*, designed to establish and maintain equality for all people regardless of race, colour, nationality or ethnic origin. As a federal law, it stands above state and territory legislation. The issue in this case was that the NTER was clearly focused on the Indigenous population.

To overcome this obvious violation of a legal statute, the federal government justified federal intervention in the Territory's affairs on the basis of what Prime Minister John Howard claimed was the unacceptable and disgraceful sexual abuse of a 'section of the Australian population'.

Critics of this development – and there have been many – pointed out that, while this claim was the public justification for sending in members of the Australian Defence Force and the Federal Police to oversee and enforce the policy, the words 'child' or 'children' did not even appear in government communiqués. Attention therefore turned to alternative explanations and justifications, leading 'many Aboriginal leaders (to) see the intervention as a land grab to make it easier for miners to access Aboriginal land'.[6]

The Intervention involved tight confinement and control – dehumanisation and suppression. Indigenous people were denied their agency and full humanity.

14.

The meaning of the land

Late in the afternoon of 29 July 2015, approximately 100 km south of Tennant Creek and 390 km north of Alice Springs, I reached Karlu Karlu, or the Devil's Marbles Conservation Reserve. I initially stopped outside the entrance for an overview of the rocks. With the sun low on the western horizon, the shapes, colours and shadows of the big boulders were magnified, and their mystique intensified. The sight was mesmerising.

To my dismay, I saw people climbing over the rocks. One person attracted my attention. They were dressed in a very visible pink top, performing handstands and cartwheels atop a large rock. Meanwhile, others could be seen assembled at lower levels and, elsewhere, near the base. From this distance, they looked like a swarm of ants. I sensed that there was something unique about the site and that this collective behaviour was wrong.

I then drove to the main tourist carpark, on the far eastern side of the reserve. It's an official camp site for trailers, campervans and others who still 'rough it' in tents. There were scores of vehicles backed into position, many with occupants sitting in chairs at the front, watching the world go by as the sun set behind the rocks. The diversity of state number plates signalled that these travellers were from all over the country. My hunch was that they were an assembly of tourists, nomads and wanderers. I had no intention of stopping to check my assumption; instead, I conducted a brief drive through the area, past all the mobile touring paraphernalia.

The way the campers had arranged themselves looked like a modern version of wagons camped in a circle to guard against a

Devils Marbles/Karlu Karlu Conservation
Reserve, NT.

night-time attack – like an updated scene from a 1950s Hollywood Western. It struck me that that the tourist carpark was a disturbing metaphor for the geo-social story of the whole nation, with the bulk of the population huddled together in urban fortresses around the coastal perimeter.

At a different cluster of rocks, but still in the same reserve, I stopped again to explore a little more of the labyrinth of natural alleys, canyons and staircases of the rock formations. When I returned to my car, two buses of school students and teachers had arrived. The educator in me was instantly activated, curious about how this part of their excursion would unfold. On disembarking, the teachers were trying to keep control, but the students quickly dispersed and headed in many different directions. There was little interest in the incredible rocks that surrounded them. Only a small number of children, with notebooks in hand, remained close to the teachers. Others formed group-huddles in little canyons between large boulders. Clearly, friendship groups were more important than this location, even with its impressive geological formations.

Here, on the perimeter of the carpark, I started to learn about the social and cultural importance of the reserve for Indigenous groups of the region. A collection of information boards provided an overview of the social history of the area as a significant sacred site. The signage also addressed my concerns. There were explicit requests for people not to climb on the rocks. Either the signs were not strategically well positioned, or people were choosing to ignore the 'do not climb' directive.

The heading of each board highlighted content that contributed to an overall Dreamtime story:

A Sacred Meeting Place; The Traditional Way

Kwerrwympe/Munga Munga Dreaming; A Women's Dreaming Story

Karlwekarlwe In the Dreamtime; The Dreaming is Still Here

Looking to the Future; Timeline from the Creation of Karlu Karlu in the Dreamtime to 2008.

Collectively, the boards provide a story about Karlu Karlu as a sacred site that holds great importance for traditional owners from four different Indigenous groups: the Warumungu, Kaytetye, Alyawarra and Warlpiri people.

Later, back in Melbourne, I conducted an extensive search for details of the reserve. The best source was a short film titled *KARLU KARLU: The Devil's Marbles* (2009), produced by the Central Australian Aboriginal Media Association team of director David Tranter and cinematographer Warwick Thornton. It dramatised the backstory to the handing back of the site to traditional owners. The film focuses on the role played by local elder Lesley Foster in that process. Here are some excerpts from Foster's statement about the handback:

> I belong here.
>
> I'm the boss of Karlu Karlu.
>
> My skin name is Pitjara.
>
> Old people used to walk around here, but they've all passed away now.
>
> I have no one left now.
>
> I am the only main one left.
>
> …
>
> I was after this country for about twenty-eight years.
>
> …
>
> I kept going to Land Council meetings and asking for this country.
>
> I kept pushing to get Karlu Karlu back.
>
> I've been fighting for twenty-eight years
>
> All the white fellas got sick of it, and they said,
>
> 'We'll have to do something'.
>
> The government people said,
>
> 'We'll have to give him back that land'.
>
> So, I went to a meeting at Hamilton Downs

And I thought, I will have my last try there

At Hamilton Downs for Karlu Karlu.

I never went to anymore meetings after that.

…

Well, they had a meeting down in Canberra

Because I was still asking for Karlu Karlu.

They thought about it and said, 'He's been asking for a long time

And he's still talking about that place.

He's still asking about Karlu Karlu.

So, we'll have to give it back to him, his country'.

And they gave it back to me all right.

They handed it back to me.

Karlu Karlu.

The process took several years. It involved discussions, debates and layers of consultations with many government officials. An excerpt from a statement provided by the Minister of Parks and Wildlife in the NT Government highlights the nature of that political and bureaucratic complexity:

Message from the Minister

The Devil's Marbles is a living cultural landscape and the traditional country of the Warumungu, Kaytetye, Warlpiri and Alyawarra peoples. Known as Karlu Karlu in all local Aboriginal languages, the Devil's Marbles are integral to the continuation of important dreamings that hold the land and its people together. Under their law, Traditional Owners have lived on, cared for, and been provided for, by this land. And, after struggling for many years to be recognised as the original and rightful owners of Karlu Karlu, the Traditional Owners were finally granted formal title to the area under the *Aboriginal Land Rights (Northern Territory) Act*, on 28 October, 2008.

The Devil's Marbles Conservation Reserve is also an important tourism attraction of the Barkly region, welcoming around 100,000 visitors each year. It is a nationally and internationally recognisable symbol of the Northern Territory's outback.

Recent changes to the *Territory Parks and Wildlife Conservation Act* bring exciting new opportunities for joint management partnerships with the Aboriginal Traditional Owners of Northern Territory parks and reserves. The Devil's Marbles Conservation Reserve is the second reserve to have a Joint Management Plan completed under these changes.[1]

This Plan recognises Traditional Owners' connection to their country under Territory law. It protects their sites, represents their aspirations for social development and facilitates their desire to be successful joint managers.

In many ways, my brief stopover at Karlu Karlu/Devils Marbles is a metaphor for mining's relationship to the land of the traditional owners. The spectacle of people climbing over the rocks signifies a broader lack of respect for the land and a refusal to properly acknowledge its guardians. The 'circled wagons' in the camping grounds typify mining management's defensive strategies in response to any attempts to curtail their activities. And the students' various responses can be seen to signify a lack of interest by the broad mining community, but with a small group who want to learn more about Indigenous people and the land.

Countering the dominant narratives

In *The Great Australian Silence*, W. E. H. Stanner argued that there is a massive gulf in understanding and language that must be bridged to confront the unresolved politics of land ownership and use in Australia.[2]

Warlpiri Elder Jerry Jangala explains that, unlike the Western attitude towards land – which sees it as something to be privately owned – many Indigenous people believe that land is for everybody.

From 23 to 26 May 2017, a group of Aboriginal and Torres Strait Islander people took part in the First Nations National Constitutional Convention. Its purpose was registering a claim for First Nations peoples to have a voice in the Australian Constitution. At its conclusion, the Convention released a document titled 'The Uluru Statement from the Heart'.

Below is a section of the Uluru Statement containing sentiments that I understand as cosmological. They indicate that Aboriginal and Torres Strait Islander peoples hold a big-picture perspective of life in the larger cosmos. As I am not, in any way, entitled to offer further interpretations, I include a central feature of the Uluru Statement in its entirety:

> We, gathered at the 2017 National Constitutional Convention, coming from all points of the southern sky, make this statement from the heart:
>
> Our Aboriginal and Torres Strait Islander tribes were the first sovereign Nations of the Australian continent and its adjacent islands and possessed it under our own laws and customs. This our ancestors did, according to the reckoning of our culture, from the Creation, according to the common law from 'time immemorial', and according to science more than 60,000 years ago.
>
> This sovereignty is a spiritual notion: the ancestral tie between the land, or 'mother nature', and the Aboriginal and Torres Strait Islander peoples who were born therefrom, remain attached thereto, and must one day return thither to be united with our ancestors.
>
> This link is the basis of the ownership of the soil, or better, of sovereignty. It has never been ceded or extinguished and co-exists with the sovereignty of the Crown.
>
> How could it be otherwise? That peoples possessed a land for sixty millennia and this sacred link disappears from world history in merely the last two hundred years?

The Uluru Statement provides a warrant to resolve the unfinished business set in motion by 200 years of colonisation of Indigenous people's land.

The first steps in that process involve developing an understanding about the meaning of land, as expressed in the Uluru Statement. This contrasts sharply with the cultural and economic practices of mining and other abominable practices justified under the banner of *terra nullius*.

An online publication by Australians Together[3] provides a clear and accessible statement about 'The importance of land', including key themes:

1. **Relationship with the land remains fundamental to the identity and way of life of many Indigenous people.** Land is much more than soil, rocks and minerals. It's a living environment that sustains, and is sustained by, people and culture.
2. **Connection to Country.** Land relates to all aspects of existence – culture, spirituality, language, law, family, and identity.
3. **The way we treat land matters.** The relationship between many Indigenous people and the land is one of reciprocity and respect – the land sustains and provides for the people, and the people sustain and manage the land through culture and ceremony.
4. **Disconnection from Country.** When non-Indigenous people begin to understand the importance of land for Indigenous people, they will appreciate why dislocation from land has had such devastating effects on many Indigenous people and cultures. Colonisation did more than steal their land, it stole their very identity.
5. **Living together on this land.** Warlpiri Elder, Jerry Jangala, explains that unlike the Western attitude towards land, which sees it as something to be privately owned, many Indigenous people believe that land is for everybody.

The following excerpts, from the work of W.E.H. Stanner, provide an appropriate concluding statement to this section.

> White man got no dreaming,
>
> Him go 'nother way.
>
> White man, him go different.
>
> Him got road belong himself.
>
> Muta, a Murinbata[4]

> White man gave no consideration to the black man's rights. The Aboriginal population was dispossessed of 'enormous areas', allowing for the creation of an immensely profitable economy based upon the exploitation of the land's natural resources.[5]

Conclusions

My mining journeys, along with endless reading and rumination, eventually led to this book. Those who have travelled with me to these concluding pages will have become acquainted with some of the enduring and emerging issues associated with the people, practices and politics of mining in Australia. What, in sum, have I shared with you?

I began with my inquiries into the shocking Morwell mine fire and its heart-wrenching fallout. So many issues arose from this event, including, who is responsible for addressing such disasters when there is no obvious locus of control in the global configuration of extraction involved? What began as a small case study of one location turned into the journeys of inquiry narrated here.

I offered an account of mining's dominant narratives and its current subordinate counter narratives, but implied, throughout, that the dominant narratives are increasingly being challenged. There is a shift underway in mining narratives; those that have been dominant are losing sway.

In the bulk of this book, I provided examples of different practices of mining in Australia. I showed how these differences are manifest in various locations and how some have changed over time. Certain locations have colossal, open pit mines requiring immensely powerful drilling equipment and giant extraction-carrying vehicles. In other locations, massive trains carry huge loads of iron ore across enormous distances from mine to port. Other mines with large-scale, deep underground extraction require highly specialised drilling technologies.

Then there are the less sophisticated, small-scale, surface level extractions. One major change is the way sophisticated technologies, deployed from afar, remotely control local sites' testing and production processes.

On a local scale, I drew out the implications and issues for workers, local communities, land misuse and rehabilitation.

Obviously, mining provides an income for workers. But working conditions have often been highly risky, resulting in severe health problems and death. FIFO workers face pressures including time away from families, isolation, sexual assault and difficulties in forming unions. In contrast, in the early 1900s, the miners in Broken Hill had no such difficulties – strikes were the norm.

Mining sites are often built on the lands of Indigenous communities, and new communities usually arise around mining sites. Racist hostilities can arise between the two. But both communities can be badly affected by aspects of local mining. Indigenous communities can be expelled from their own land – perhaps to the margins of local townships. Townships can be hollowed out when miners who live locally are replaced by FIFO workers. And when mining sites close, towns may decline, despite local attempts to reinvent them. Other problems include poor living conditions, poor health associated with toxic spill-over and poor air quality. And local communities often feel that they have lost control of their own affairs.

As an industry, mining shows no respect for the land as such or for Indigenous people's land ownership. Indeed, the State and mining companies often combine forces to take possession of Indigenous land. The mining industry only respects the wealth that can be extracted from land. Further, it uses, and wastes, water at will, as various examples of the ugly scars on the landscape that mining leaves behind show. Overburden is an understatement. Mining is usually undertaken without conscience or care. Adequate rehabilitation plans rarely accompany mine closures. And such plans, when implemented, can be very short sighted in terms of their geophysical consequences.

This book addressed some of the implications and issues on a broader scale – particularly the extent and power of global configurations of extraction. These have global chains of production, supply and consumption and include ENGIE, Rio Tinto, BHP, CBH Resources, ZhonLingnan Mining, Saracen Mining and Alcoa. Ownership and management are invariably at a distance. Extractivism, as identified by Klein, is their norm. It is part and parcel of what Birch sees as the co-dependent relationship between colonialism and capitalism. Extractivism is evident in each mining location described here – the taking without caring, the objectification of labour and nature and the associated production of sacrifice zones.

In remote locations, not only mining is involved in land use, misuse and abuse. Others share with mining a *terra nullius* mindset. Examples discussed illustrate the role of the State in such maltreatment. For the State, the notion of *terra nullius* permits harm, secrecy and coverup in remote locations. In the NT, the settler colonial and the carceral State implemented the Intervention and the associated horrors.

There is no doubt that global configurations of extraction are implicated in the problem of global climate change and that their approach to the land is a causal factor. Chapter 14 offered an alternative understanding of the land, drawn from Australia's Indigenous people. This poses a direct challenge to mining's dominant practices and narratives.

There are two updates to the stories told here: what is happening at Morwell and the Hazelwood power station; and some recent developments in the wider world of mining as concerns about climate change intensify.

A post-mining transition begins

Following the 2014 open pit fire, anxiety grew within many sectors of Morwell's extended community. Messages filtering out of the power company headquarters in Paris did not bode well for the future. ENGIE made it clear, through its global publicity system, that it was moving away from traditional forms of fossil fuel production and towards renewable energy systems. While ENGIE focused on trends in the global marketplace that were constantly being adjusted in tune with developments in climate change science and political shifts, individual community members of Morwell and associated towns had to deal with multiple levels of uncertainty about the future.

Local and state government officials have been visible in the transition period, working to dampen down and stabilise the general anxiety about current uncertainties and problems and to chart a course towards a post-mining future.

In the first instance, municipal leaders of the Latrobe Valley encountered struggles and challenges on multiple fronts. Some individuals and families who experienced the loss of work and identity needed assistance. Financial and personal hardship went hand in hand. A range of local Emergency Relief Services assisted individuals and families to deal with their immediate needs.

Serious soul searching about the long-term economic viability of the region was needed. The previously dominant power industry was in wind-down, and alternative industries were needed, with a new economic and employment plan and narrative. Councillor Middlemiss' words are pertinent:

> The town's spirit didn't die. The fact is lots of jobs went, but it didn't knock the town about anywhere near as much as people thought... Brown coal power generation economy is on its way out... We have to transform our economy to find alternatives...about 150 jobs would be created through the state government hub... The government has just announced this electric vehicle delivery factory for 100 jobs.[1]

The hub he mentions involves the state government's engagement in establishing a post-mining local economy. Its first stage will be the construction of a $30 million, three-storey building in Morwell to foster economic growth, attract new industries and create a range of employment in the public and private sectors. An initial proposal is to establish an industrial park for industries such as food and fibre, manufacturing, heavy industry and associated auxiliary services.

In 2016, during the height of uncertainty about Hazelwood power station's viability, unemployment peaked at 10.6 percent.

In 2021, that figure had fallen to 7.9 percent. While still relatively high, the most recent figures are tangible evidence of the improving economic health of the region; it is trending in a positive direction.

The closure of Hazelwood raises the question of what to do with the 4,000-hectare site. In June 2019, ENGIE released a Concept Master Plan for the rehabilitation of the abandoned mine void, stating:

> ENGIE has identified preferred landforms for each of the elements of the site, which include:
>
> – filling the mine void with water 'the full lake scenario' (assessed to be the lowest risk scenario with regard to safety and stability, and possible future opportunities).[2]

This plan involves diverting the Morwell River through the former mine, to fill the pit.

Predictably, there are several concerns with this proposal. The eventual lake would have a volume of 600 gigalitres, greater than the volume of Sydney Harbour at approximately 500 GL. Hydrology studies suggest that a lake of this size – coupled with two similar storages once Yallourn and Loy Yang power stations close – would change the microclimate of the region. The overflow from the lakes, back into the larger Latrobe River, would contain a mix of chemical sediments from the former mines, and this altered water would then have downstream effects for irrigators of central and East Gippsland and then for the quality of water flowing into the larger Gippsland Lake complex. Local and state officials, representatives from ENGIE and several environment protection groups are currently addressing these wide-ranging matters.

This mix of concerns provides a valuable insight into the complexity of the considerations required to deal safely, environmentally and ethically with the giant voids left from closed mines. In Australia, that matter has not yet been adequately addressed.

How dirty is clean energy?

As the discourse of a decarbonised economy begins to take hold, powerful global corporations are reshaping their supply chains to be at the head of the pack as suppliers of clean products.

The emergence of electric vehicles (EVs) is a case in point. Columnist Daniel Mercer has noted the changes in the supply chains that link growing consumer demand for clean private vehicles with the associated extraction and production of the minerals needed for the alternative fuel supplies to power EVs:

> Commodity giant Glencore is in the thick of the action, operating battery minerals mines across the country. At its Murrin Murrin mine, about 800km north-east of Perth in Western Australia's Goldfields, the Swiss-Anglo company is producing nickel and cobalt to help feed demand from automakers.

> ... Across the world, the uptake of electric vehicles, or EVs, is accelerating as car makers and consumers embrace the technology and governments seek to decarbonise transport ... Australia is definitely at the head of the pack when it comes to mineral endowment.

> ... While lithium is the best known of the critical minerals – lending its name to the high-performance batteries typical of EVs – a slew of other materials are also required. Among them are nickel, cobalt, manganese, vanadium, zinc and copper – all of which are found in abundance in Australia.[3]

Clarification is required about the precise meaning of the category 'critical minerals'. This is a catch phrase; 'critical' has long been used to describe the resources required by a society to fuel its economy at a particular time. Coal was deemed to be 'critical' during Europe's industrial revolution. In post-industrial, high-tech societies, 'critical' resources are those needed to power and manage an increasingly complex amalgam of devices and systems, including:

- Artificial Intelligence and Machine Learning
- Robotic Process Automation
- Edge Computing
- Quantum Computing
- Virtual Reality and Augmented Reality
- Blockchain
- Internet of Things
- 5G
- Cybersecurity

This list highlights the far-reaching evolution of new technologies and interconnected systems that, in turn, increase the demand for the appropriate rare earth elements deemed 'critical minerals'.

In *The Rare Metals War*, Guillaume Pitron fills out the details of this caveat with example after example of the messes that have been left behind in former mine sites, the hidden costs of extraction of tiny amounts of rare earth minerals during large-scale production processes and the lack of conscientious 'ground-truthing' safeguards caused by the enthusiasm for, and preoccupation with, generating profit.[4] His expansive and detailed analyses provide a timely reminder that environmental costs must be part of the wider conversation about extractive processes and that human needs and desires are far outpacing the earth's capacity to recover and regenerate. While enormous efforts and energy are expended on reducing greenhouse gases in the atmosphere, pollution is being 'displaced to the areas where the resources needed for this very technology are mined',[5] and 'the globalisation of supply chains gives us consumer goods while taking away knowledge of their origin.'[6]

Foley and Toscano note:

> Australia's energy market operator is preparing for more coal-fired power stations to close many years earlier than planned and expects all of Victoria's coal plants to be shut by 2032, demanding a massive expansion of renewable energy and 10,000 extra kilometres of power lines to connect the grid.[7]

Further, Clun[8] has argued that Australia is quickly becoming the targeted source for 'critical materials' which are the building blocks of new and alternative forms of energy. As a large area, containing many different forms of minerals, Australia is increasingly primed to be a major global player in this shift to renewable energy. A new quarry for the world, perhaps.

I wonder whether all the hype around critical minerals' clean, green credentials is just an example of what Klein calls 'magical thinking'. Given the growing urgency and demand for alternative resources, will many of the destructive practices of the past be repeated? In the race to capture a share of the renewables market, will they be located, extracted, refined, processed and commodified in ways that do not involve extractivism?

There are many compelling words of warning. Perhaps the most dangerous and volatile scenario is what Pitron describes as the 'race for precision-guided missiles'.[9] Currently, several countries are engaged in major military conflicts, most seriously the struggle that began with a Russian attack on Ukraine in February 2022. Russia launched ballistic missiles then subsequently began using Shahed-136 drones as the weapon of choice.

This perilous and deadly conflict, involving the use of high-tech weapons, is very relevant within the story of mining and the recent focus on rare earth metals. These alloys have become vital ingredients of military arsenals. Pitron notes:

> Every time a people, civilisation, or state masters a new metal, it leads to exponential technical and military progress and deadlier conflicts. Now it is rare metals and in particular rare earths, that are changing the face of modern warfare.[10]

The relevance of this trend for mining in Australia becomes more complex and politically significant when we consider that, until recently, China has been the major source of the rare earth minerals that are increasingly important in the production of modern missiles and military deployment and surveillance systems. Within the context of the emergent superpower struggle between China and the USA, Australia has become an important alternative site in the militarised supply chain.

Here, the fight against global warming comes up against geo-political battles. Both are caught up in the ongoing competition between large corporations for marketplace supremacy.

This moment of transformation away from the use of fossil fuels and towards renewables must involve genuinely sustainable and ethical practices. For such change to occur, the world of mining needs to develop a very different mindset and apply it to more than the transition from fossil fuels to alternative renewable sources. The processes and procedures across the entirety of the power production supply chain must also change. The mining of critical minerals must properly and fairly consider, and learn from, Indigenous people's relationships to the land.

The dirty life of mining in this country offers some salutary lessons. My collection of small case studies shows how the land has been disturbed, deposited elsewhere, damaged, polluted and poisoned. The mining mentality has carried over into other land use practices, including one area that was bombed and 'nuked'. This has happened to such an extent that ancient patterns, flows and physical structures have been shattered, broken apart and used up. They have disappeared from popular memory. Consequently, most of the land described here needs repair, recovery, rehabilitation, restoration and greater respect. As we adopt alternative ways of living sustainably, we must develop a genuine sense of equity that reaches beyond the avaricious, human-centred history of previous production practices. Unequivocally, mining's dominant narrative of extraction-as-progress has an unhappy ending.

Endnotes

Introduction

1 *Supersized Earth: The Story of our Manmade World* [television documentary], Producers R. Sharman, R. Liddell and N. Walk, British Broadcasting Corporation, 2014.

2 *Supersized Earth*, Episode 3, 'Food, fire and water'.

3 Gambrenk Mining Engineering blog, 'Introduction to mining', 5 August 2010, https://gambrenk-miningengineering.blogspot.com/search?q=introduction+to+mining (accessed 16 April 2022).

4 J. Zubrzycki, *Settlers of the Latrobe Valley*, Australian National University, 1964.

5 P. Carter, *Ground Truthing: Explorations in a Creative Region*, UWA, 2010, p. 282.

6 Carter, *Ground Truthing*, p. 290.

7 E. Abbey, *Desert Solitaire: A Season in the Wilderness*, Simon & Schuster, 1968, p. xiv.

8 G. Fleming, D. Merrett and S. Ville, *The Big End of Town: Big Business and Corporate Leadership in Twentieth-Century Australia*, Cambridge University Press, 2004.

9 Michael Roche, Global Energy Monitor, https://www.gem.wiki/Michael_Roche (accessed 5 September 2022).

10 S. Ville, *Resilience and Fragility in the Asian Century: Refocusing Australia's economic narratives through the lens of economic history*, Academy of Social Sciences in Australia Keith Hancock Lecture 2014, Academy Papers 1/2015.

Part 1

1 World Economic Forum, Introduction to *The Global Risks Report 2017*, 12th ed. https://www3.weforum.org/docs/GRR17_Report_web.pdf (accessed 6 November 2022).

Chapter 1: Choking on smoke

1   'Herald Sun photographer Jason Edwards captures images of the fire emergency in Morwell', *Herald Sun*, 10 February 2014, https://www.heraldsun.com.au/news/victoria/herald-sun-photographer-jason-edwards-captures-images-of-the-fire-emergency-in-morwell/news-story/bbb4a02dc812b2dee53d4371cd92d750.

2   M.L. Yueyang and S. McDill, 'Australian coal mine fire burning for three weeks', Reuters, Mining and Communities database, 2014 (accessed 5 March 2022).

3   E. Ferguson, 'In Gratitude, Hazelwood Mine Fire, Board of Inquiry', *CFA News & Media blog*, Country Fire Authority, 23 March 2014 (accessed 30 May 2022).

Chapter 2: Shifting blame

1   ABC News, *'Election results – Morwell',* Victoria Votes, 2020 (accessed 22 July 2017).

2   D. Andrews, 'Hazelwood Mine Fire Inquiry Reopened' [media release], Victorian State Government, 26 May 2015 (accessed 22 July 2017).

3   C. Doutré, 'Hazelwood coal mine fire report tabled at Victorian Parliament today', *The Weekly Times*, 3 September 2014 (accessed 5 March 2020).

4   T. Arup, 'Hazelwood owners GDF Suez refusing to pay $18 million mine fire bill', *The Age*, 6 July 2015 (accessed 22 July 2017).

5   ENGIE, 'GDF SUEZ becomes ENGIE', media release, 24 April 2015 (accessed 22 July 2017).

Part 2

Chapter 3: Australian mining

1   J.P. Casey, 'Super mines: Australia's biggest mining projects', *Mine Australia Magazine*, issue 4, 2019 (accessed 15 April 2022).

2   Casey, 'Super mines'.

3   International Mining and Resources Conference (IMARC) *2nd Annual International Mining and Resources Conference: Post Event Report*, IMARC, 9 12 November 2015, Melbourne Convention and Exhibition Centre (accessed 14 April 2022).

4 G. Blainey, 'Mining and the Australian people – the long view'; Conference Keynote, International Mining and Resources Conference (IMARC) 2015, *2nd Annual International Mining and Resources Conference: Post Event Report*, IMARC, 9–12 November 2015, Melbourne Convention and Exhibition Centre.

5 N. Klein, *This Changes Everything: Capitalism vs. the Climate*, Simon & Schuster, 2014.

6 G. Blainey, *The Peaks of Lyell*, Melbourne University Press, 1954.

7 G. Blainey, *The Rush That Never Ended: A History of Australian Mining*, Melbourne University Press, 2003.

8 M. Knox, *Boom: The Underground History of Australia, from Gold Rush to GFC*, Penguin, 2013.

9 Australian Government Department of the Prime Minister and Cabinet, *Australian National Colours*, n.d. (accessed 15 April 2022).

10 J. Nieuwenhuysen, 'Foreword', in Jon Altman and David Martin (eds), *Power, Culture, Economy: Indigenous Australians and Mining*, ANU Press, 1984, p. ix.

11 https://www.goldfifieldsguide.com.au/explore-location/281/new-australasian-no-2-gold-mine/ (accessed 29 Oct 2022).

12 F. Cahir, *Black Gold: Aboriginal People on the Goldfields of Victoria, 1850–1870*, ANU Press, 2012.

Chapter 4: Critical considerations

1 Klein, *This Changes Everything*, 2014.

2 Klein, *This Changes Everything*, p. 360.

3 Klein, *This Changes Everything*, p. 169.

4 Klein, *This Changes Everything*, p. 311.

5 Klein, *This Changes Everything*, p. 310.

6 Klein, *This Changes Everything*, pp. 294–309.

7 Klein, *This Changes Everything*, p. 295.

8 Klein, *This Changes Everything*, p. 370.

9 Klein, *This Changes Everything*, pp. 254–255.

10 Klein, *This Changes Everything*, p. 252.

11 Klein, *This Changes Everything*, pp. 186–187.

12 N. Klein, *The Shock Doctrine: The Rise of Disaster Capitalism*, Picador, 2007.

13 Klein, *This Changes Everything*, p. 25.

14 Klein, *This Changes Everything*, p. 407.

15 T. Birch, '"History is Never Bloodless"; Getting it Wrong after One Hundred Years of Federation', *Australian Historical Studies*, vol. 33, no. 118, 2002, pp. 42–53; T. Birch, '"I'm not sure how to begin it": The Welcome Uncertainties of Doing History' in T. Neale, C. McKinnon & E. Vincent (eds) *History, Power, Text: Cultural Studies and Indigenous Studies*, CTR books, 2014.

16 T. Birch, '"We've Seen the End of the World and We don't Accept it": Protection of Indigenous Country and Climate Justice', in J. Camilleri and D. Guess (eds), *Towards a Just and Ecologically Sustainable Peace: Navigating the Great Transition*, Palgrave Macmillan, 2020, 257.

17 T. Birch, '"We've Seen the End of the World and We don't Accept it": Protection of Indigenous Country and Climate Justice', in N. Oke, C. Sonn and A. Baker (eds), *Places of privilege: Interdisciplinary perspectives on identities, change and resistance*, BRILL, 2018, p. 141.

18 T. Birch, 'Climate Change, Mining and Traditional Indigenous Knowledge', in *Australia, Social Inclusion*, vol. 4, no. 1, 2016, p. 95.

19 T. Birch, '"On what terms can we speak?" Refusal, resurgence and climate justice', transcript of Duguid memorial lecture 2018, *Coolabah*, nos. 24–25, 2018, pp. 2–16.

20 T. Birch, '"We've Seen the End of the World and We don't Accept it": Protection of Indigenous Country and Climate Justice', in N. Oke, C. Sonn and A. Baker (eds), *Places of privilege: Interdisciplinary perspectives on identities, change and resistance*, BRILL, 2018, p. 8.

Part 3

Chapter 5: Poisonous Legacies

1 C. Adams, 'The Silver City: A Medical History', *Barrier Daily Truth*, 2 May 2017 (accessed 12 March 2022).

2 B. Walker, *Solidarity Forever: a Part Story of the Life and Time of Percy*

Laidler – the First Quarter of a Century, National Press, 1972, https://
www.solidarityforeverbook.com

3   B. O'Neil, 'The BHP Lockout of 1909: the View from Three
    Generations of Broken Hill Miners', *Journal of Australasian Mining
    History,* vol. 10, October 2012 (accessed 12 March 2022).

4   S.J. Brennan, *'The Legacy of Justice Higgins: Seeking a True New Start
    for all Job Seekers and Workers'*, PM Glynn Institute, Australian
    Catholic University, 2017 (accessed 12 March 2022).

5   M.R. Kersten, *'Broken Hill Trade Unionism',* Full Day Hansard
    Transcript, Parliament of New South Wales, 1997. Archived from
    the original on 24 September 2015 (accessed 14 August 2015).

6   S. Bloodworth, 'Broken Hill: A Radical History', *Red Flag*, 2015
    (accessed 12 March 2022).

7   P. Dwyer & M. Walker, "Patrick 'Bunny" Dwyer interviewed by
    Murray Walker', in *Murray Walker collection on Australian country
    life* (sound recording), 1980.

8   'Patrick "Bunny" Dwyer interviewed by Murray Walker'.

9   C. Dong, M.P. Taylor, L.K. Kristensen, & S. Zahran, 'Environmental
    contamination in an Australian mining community and potential
    influences on early childhood health and Behavioural outcomes,'
    Environmental Pollution', no. 207, 2015, pp. 345–356, https://doi.
    org/10.1016/j.envpol.2015.09.037

10 C. Armitage, 'Australia's most dangerous streets revealed by school
    testing,' *Sydney Morning Herald*, 8 October 2015 (accessed 13 March
    2022).

11 Armitage, 'Australia's most dangerous streets'.

12 *Mining History; Broken Hill – 11/269/20*, Broken Hill Library
    Production.

13 Macquarie University, ' Lead smelter still exposing Port Pirie
    children to unacceptable levels of pollution', *The Lighthouse,*
    https://lighthouse.mq.edu.au/media-releases/lead-smelter-
    still-exposing-port-pirie-children-to-unacceptable-levels-of-
    pollution (accessed 30 October 2022). Full study: M. P. Taylor,
    C. Isley and J. Glover, 'Prevalence of childhood lead poisoning
    and respiratory disease associated with lead smelter emissions.'
    Environmental International, March 2019. https://doi.org/10.1016/j.
    envint.2019.01.062

14 CBH Resources Limited, 'Company overview', 2022 (accessed 13 March 2022).

15 Perilya (n.d.) History; Perilya (accessed 13 March 2022).

Chapter 6: Pillaging water

1 BHP, *Olympic Dam Investment creates foundation for the future*, 2018, (accessed 18 March 2022).

2 *Roxby Downs (Indenture Ratification) Act, 1982* (No 52 f 1982), June 1982, http://inis.iaea.org/search/search.aspx?orig_q=RN:14788727 (accessed 6 November 2022).

3 C. Torrisi & P. Trotta, 'Sustainable water use at Olympic Dam', *Mining Technology*, vol. 118, no. 3–4, 2009, pp. 193–204, 10.1179/174328610X12682159814984_

4 Friends of the Earth Australia (n.d.), *Olympic Dam – Summary of Major Concerns* (accessed 18 March 2022).

5 Wikipedia, *Olympic Dam Mine* (accessed 18 March 2022).

6 Climate Data, 'Roxby Downs Climate', https://en.climate-data.org/oceania/australia/south-australia/roxby-downs-764904/ (accessed 1 September 2022).

Chapter 7: Rough cuts

1 T. Winton, Foreward, *Rhythms of the Kimberley: A Seasonal Journey Through Australia's North* by Russell Gueho, Fremantle Press, 2007, p. 9.

2 Bureau of Meteorology, *Climate Statistics for Australian Locations*, 2022 (accessed 18 March 2022).

3 Rio Tinto (2021) *'Argyle'* (accessed 18 March 2022).

4 Rio Tinto, *Rio Tinto dazzles New York with its rare red and pink diamonds*, 3 October 2019, (accessed 6 October 2022).

5 Rio Tinto, *Rio Tinto dazzles New York*.

6 Rio Tinto, *Rio Tinto dazzles New York*.

7 K. Marx, *Capital: Volume 1: A Critique of Political Economy*, Neeland Media, 1867 and 2010.

Chapter 8: Technological behemoth

1 Academic Dictionaries and Encyclopedias, Mount Newman Railway, https://En-Academic.com, (accessed 9 August 2022).

2 BHP, *'BHP Billiton Iron Ore Western Australian Overview'*, 2013 (accessed 26 March 2022).

3 Shire of East Pilbara, *Shire of East Pilbara*, 2017 (accessed 26 March 2022).

4 Australian Bureau of Statistics, 2021 Census. Newman: 2021 Census all persons quick stats. Search results | Australian Bureau of Statistics, abs.gov.au (accessed 9 August 2022).

5 R. Parish, 'Kurra Village dongas dismantled as BHP closes Pilbara FIFO camp after three-year delay', *ABC News,* 2020 (accessed 26 March 2022).

6 Commonwealth of Australia, *Cancer of the bush or salvation for our cities? Fly-in, fly-out and drive-in, drive-out workforce practices in Regional Australia*, House of Representatives Standing Committee on Regional Australia, 2013 (accessed 26 March 2022).

7 House of Representatives Standing Committee on Regional Australia, Media Release, *Regional Australia Committee issues key FIFO report*, 2013 https _ _ _ aphref.aph.gov.au _ house _ committee _ ra _ fifodido _ media _ media25.pdf (accessed 1 January 2020)

8 Australian Mining Cities Alliance, *Ten Years on and still no cure for Cancer of the Bush (FIFO)*, media release, 2021 (accessed 26 March 2022).

9 ACMA, *Ten Years on and still no cure for Cancer of the Bush (FIFO)*.

10 V. Meredith, P. Rush and E. Robinson (2014) 'Fly-in fly-out workforce practices in Australia: The effects on children and family relationships', CFCA PAPER NO. 19, Australian Institute of Family Studies (accessed 26 March 2022).

11 Government of Western Australia, Department of Mines, *Industry Regulation and Safety Codes of Practice*, February 2022.

12 Department of Mines, Industry Regulation and Safety, *Mentally healthy workplaces for fly-in-fly-out (FIFO) workers in the resources and construction sector*, https://www.google.com.au/search?q=Mentally+healthy+workplaces+for+fly-in-fly-out+%28FIFO%29+workers+in+the+resources+and+construction+sector (accessed 31 October 2022).

13 A. Vassiley, *'From 'Union Power' to De-unionisation: Explaining the Rise and Fall of Trade Unionism in Western Australia's Pilbara Iron Ore Industry and its Consequences'*, PhD thesis, Curtin University, 2021, p. 315.

14 N. Toscano, 'Rise of the machines: Why Australia's miners are racing for automation', *Sydney Morning Herald*, 30 November 2019 (accessed 26 March 2022).

15 V. Zhou, 'BHP plots massive automation roll out across Australia', *Australian Mining*, 26 July 2019 (accessed 1 April 2022).

16 M.P. Juanola, 'Welcome to the slums on the very edge of WA's mining epicentre', *WA Today*, MP 19 June 2019 (accessed 26 March 2022).

Chapter 9: 'Grinding poverty alongside relative affluence'

1 S. Gregson, 'War, Racism and Industrial Relations in an Australian Mining Town, 1916–1935', *The Economic and Labour Relations Review*, vol. 18, no. 1, 2007, pp. 79–97, https://doi.org/10.1177/103530460701800105

2 Golden Quest Discovery Trail, *Kalgoorlie–Boulder*, 2022 (accessed 1 April 2022).

3 T. Joyner, *'Residents hanging on as gold mining giant blasts beneath them spark fears'*, *ABC News*, 23 May 2018 (accessed 1 April 2022).

4 C. Bembridge, *'Kalgoorlie protest: Community mourns as elders call for action'*, *ABC News*, 30 August 2016 (accessed 1 April 2022).

5 M. Krakouer and G. Georgatos, 'Blak lives betrayed – Elijah Doughty', *National Indigenous Times*, 8 June 2020 (accessed 1 April 2022).

6 S. Standen and T. Joyner, *'Squalid homes demolished, residents relocated from Aboriginal reserves, in shadow of big-money mines'*, ABC News, 13 July 2019 (accessed 1 April 2022).

7 KPMG, *Kalgoorlie Consolidated Gold Mines (KCGM) Social Impact Assessment*, 2020, Appendix D - Part 1 - Social Impact Assessment.pdf (epa.wa.gov.au) (accessed 15 May 2022).

8 S. Standen and T. Joyner, *'Squalid homes demolished, residents relocated from Aboriginal reserves, in shadow of big-money mines'*, ABC News, 13 July 2019 (accessed 1 April 2022).

9   *What are Lynas' plans for Kalgoorlie?* https://lynasrareearths.com/
wp-content/uploads/2022/07/Lynas-Kalgoorlie-Processing-Facility-
FAQs-July-2022.pdf

Chapter 10: Closure and rehabilitation

1   Environment Victoria, '*Anglesea coal mine closure plans unveiled
under Freedom of Information*', media release, 19 August 2015
(accessed 13 May 2022).

2   Environmental Justice Australia, *Community briefing: Hazelwood
mine rehab. Learn how you can help shape Victoria's biggest
rehabilitation project*, 14 June 2022, https://envirojustice.org.au/
blog/onlineaction/hazelwood-rehab-community-briefing/

3   S. Miles, *Government Continues To Manage Texas Silver Mine*, 20
April, 2016, https://statements.qld.gov.au/statements/77746

4   K. Pacey and A. Brosnan, *Final statutory guideline for Queensland's
environmental chain of responsibility laws released*, 2017, Clayton Utz.

5   M. Willacy, *Rehabilitating abandoned mines could create thousands of
'badly needed' jobs, report says*, ABC News, 23 October 2016 (accessed 5
August 2022).

6   Environment Victoria, 'Anglesea coal mine closure plans unveiled
under Freedom of Information', media release, 19 August 2015
(accessed 13 May 2022).

7   Smit, T (2022) 'Eden's Mission', *The Eden Project*, accessed 13 May
2022

Part 4

Chapter 11: Life in remote regions

1   ABS Census (accessed 1 August 2022).

2   SA Government, 'Historical Gold Mines', Energy and Mining
(accessed 18 April 2022).

3   'Description of the Route and Locality', *Argus,* no. 12, 582, 22
October 1886, p. 6.

Chapter 12: *Terra nullius* mindsets

1   Northern Territory Government, 'Discovery and exploration',
Department of Industry, Tourism and Trade (accessed 24 April
2022).

2 F. Walker, *Maralinga*, Hachette, 2014, pp. 7–8.

3 F. Walker, *Maralinga*, p. 295.

4 F. Walker, *Maralinga*, p. 296.

5 Australian Ionising Radiation Advisory Council, *Radiological Safety and Future Land Use at the Emu Atomic Weapons Test Site*, Government Publishing Service, 1980.

6 F. Walker, *Maralinga*, p. 74.

7 J.R. McLelland, *Royal Commission into British Nuclear Tests in Australia* [Parliamentary paper No. 482/1985], Government Publishing Service, 1985.

Chapter 13: Wounded land

1 Arabana Country, *http://www.arabana.com.au* (accessed 28 September 2022).

2 *The importance of land; Source: Meaning of land to Aboriginal people – Creative Spirits*, https://www.creativespirits.info/aboriginalculture/land/meaning-of-land-to-aboriginal-people (accessed 28 September 2020).

3 https://www.opalsdownunder.com.au/learn/how-is-opal-valued/

4 M. Brough, *National emergency response to protect Aboriginal children in the NT*, media release, 12 June 2007 (accessed 29 April 2022).

5 M. Brough, *National emergency response*.

6 'Northern Territory Emergency Response (NTER) - "The Intervention"', https://www.creativespirits.info/aboriginalculture/politics/northern-territory-emergency-response-intervention#fn10 (accessed 2 October 2022).

Chapter 14: The meaning of the land

1 Parks and Wildlife Service of the Northern Territory, *Devil's Marbles (Karlu Karlu) Conservation Reserve: Joint Management Plan*, 2009 (accessed 6 May 2022).

2 W.E.H. Stanner, *White Man Got No Dreaming: Essays, 1938–1973*, Australian National University, 1979.

3 Australians Together, *The Importance of Land*, 2022 (accessed 5

August 2022).

4   Stanner, *White Man Got No Dreaming*, frontispiece.

5   W. G. Spence, *Australia's Awakening: Thirty Years in the Life of an Australian Agitator*, Worker Trustees, Sydney and Melbourne, 1909, p. 11.

Conclusions

1   M, Heagney, 'How Morwell survived the closure of its major industry and is starting to grow again', *Domain*, 5 January, 2019. https://www.domain.com.au/news/coal-to-cool-how-morwell-has-survived-and-thrived-793212/-. (accessed 27 October 2022).

2   *Hazelwood Rehabilitation: What is the Concept Master Plan*? https://engie.com.au/sites/default/files/2021-06/Concept_Master_Plan_-_Final%20Issue_sm.pdf (accessed 27 October 2022).

3   D. Mercer, '*As EVs drive a mining revolution, will Australia become a battery minerals superpower?*' ABC News, 25 August 2022, (accessed 29 September 2022).

4   G. Pitron, *The Rare Metals War: the dark side of clean energy and digital technologies*, Scribe, 2020, p. 53.

5   Pitron, *The Rare Metals War*, p. 81.

6   Pitron, *The Rare Metals War*, p.69.

7   M. Foley and N. Toscano, '"Act now": Grid chief urges renewable boom as early coal closures loom', *The Age*, 30 June 2022, https://www.theage.com.au/politics/federal/act-now-grid-chief-urges-renewable-boom-as-early-coal-closures-loom-20220629-p5axjj.html (accessed 30 June 2022).

8   R. Clun, 'European Union looks to Australia over Russia for critical materials', *Sydney Morning Herald*, 30 June 2022 (accessed 30 June 2022).

9   Pitron, *The Rare Metals War*, p. 111.

10 Pitron, *The Rare Metals War*, p. 141.

About Interventions

Interventions is an independent, not-for-profit, incorporated publisher. We publish left-wing, radical and socialist books by Australian authors. We welcome books which for political or financial reasons are unlikely to be accepted by commercial publishers. Our books cover a wide range of topics including labour history, left-wing politics, radical cultural themes, socialism and Marxism, memoirs, and works about resistance to racism, sexism and all other forms of oppression.

At Interventions we believe radical ideas matter. We want our books to be part of the development of a critical and engaged Australian left.

By highlighting alternative voices, especially those that have been pushed to the margins, we hope to contribute to a greater insight and awareness of the injustices that exist in society, and the many efforts at the grassroots to right these wrongs.

We welcome publishing proposals. If you are interested in submitting a proposal please check out the information for authors on our website https://interventions.org.au/forauthors. If you think your proposal fits our guidelines please follow the submission process outlined there. Please note we are not currently publishing poetry or fiction.

Interventions has no independent source of income and is committed to keeping prices accessible. As bookshops and warehouses close around the world, our future hangs in the balance. By supporting us you will help us keep radical ideas alive and accessible to all. If you would like to support radical publishing in Australia please consider supporting our Patreon. Visit patreon.com/interventions to donate a small amount each month and get some great rewards.

Website: https://interventions.org.au/

Contact us: info@interventions.org.au or use the contact form on the website.

About this book

The Interventions editor and production project manager for this book was Lisa Milner with support from Janey Stone. This book was copy edited by Eris Harrison of Effective Editing. This book was designed and laid out by Viktoria Ivanova. Viktoria is a communication designer in Melbourne. She is a book publishing fiend, runs Spark Publishing Inc (for art-centric left books) and also designs for Victorian Socialists.

Radical Perth, Militant Fremantle
Edited by Charlie Fox,
Alexis Vassiley, Bobbie Oliver, and
Lenore Layman

Radical Perth, Militant Fremantle tells 34 fascinating stories of
radical moments In the cities' past, from as long ago as the 1890s
and as recent as Occupy: the revolutionary theatre of the Workers
Art Guild; the riot of unemployed workers outside the Treasury
building; rock concerts inside St Georges Cathedral; bodgies and
widgies cutting up the dance floor at the Scarborough Beach Snake
Pit; the Point Peron women's peace camp, and many more.

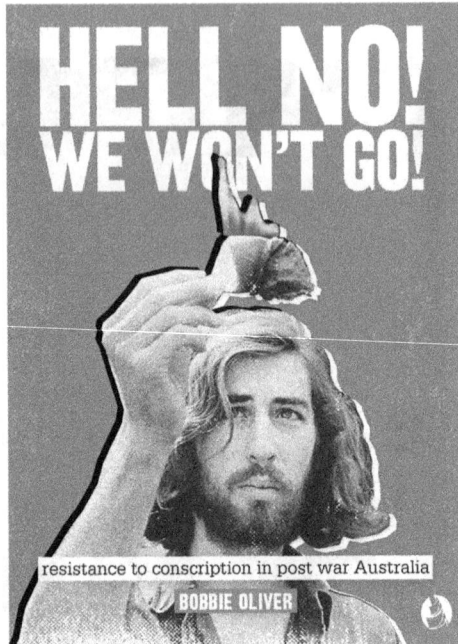

Hell no! We won't go!
Postwar resistance to conscription
in Australia
By Bobbie Oliver

Using court records and private correspondence as well as newspaper accounts, Hell no! We won't go! records the stories of many young men who resisted the National Service schemes of 1951-59, and 1965-72

Some became well-known; others were known only to family and friends. The book describes their experiences in court, in prison and underground in hiding. It also recounts their triumphs such as the great Moratorium campaigns of 1970 and 1971, the Melbourne University commune, the street marches and sit-ins, and the courage they exhibited in taking a stand that was often branded as cowardice.

In recounting these stories, Bobbie Oliver asks: What motivated them to take an unpopular stance - even to the extent of prison? What experiences and sufferings did they undergo? Did making a stand against militarism and war make a difference to society or change their lives?

MORE FROM INTERVENTIONS

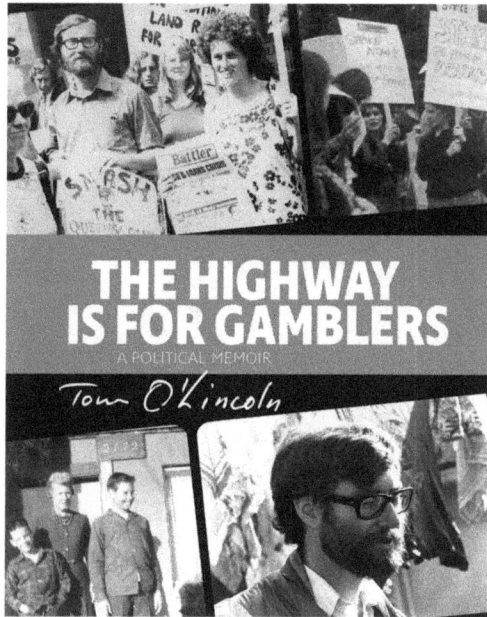

The Highway is for Gamblers:
A political memoir
By Tom O'Lincoln with Janey Stone
Introduction by Janey Stone

Tom O'Lincoln's moving political memoir is a testament to a life worth living, in the ranks of those fighting for human liberation. Tom became politicised in the turbulent 1960s and spent decades writing, organising and travelling in a lifelong effort to renew a creative tradition of Marxism in Australia and abroad.

Everyone's story is an interesting whole in its own right, and this book is what Tom has made of his - but it also captures the rich political history of the past six decades. The German student movement, Berkeley radicalism, the Whitlam sacking, the Portuguese and Nicaraguan Revolutions, the Lebanese civil war, dissidence in the Eastern bloc, labour struggles in South Korea, the fall of Suharto - many such episodes are told as eyewitness accounts, amid Tom's reflections on building the International Socialist tradition in Australia. This account of the hands-on building of the Australian radical left, alongside momentous historical global events, is written with a pen that burns with indignation against oppression. Importantly, this is not a nostalgic memoir of reminiscence, but rather an insight for the activists of tomorrow who hope to change the world.

MORE FROM INTERVENTIONS